# ROYAL MONASTERY OF EL ESCORIAL

**Text by: M.ª Teresa Ruiz Alcón**

Diagramming and reproduction by the technical staff of
EDITORIAL ESCUDO DE ORO, S.A. with the collaboration
of the Patrimonio Nacional.

Co-edition of EDITORIAL ESCUDO DE ORO, S.A. and the
PATRIMONIO NACIONAL.

1st Edition, June 1987

I.S.B.N.

| | |
|---|---|
| Spanish | 84-378-1221-6 |
| French | 84-378-1222-4 |
| English | 84-378-1223-2 |
| German | 84-378-1224-0 |
| Italian | 84-378-1225-9 |

Dep. Legal B. 23448-1987

 **escudo de oro, s.a.** Palaudarias, 26 - 08004 Barcelona - Spain

Impreso en España - Printed in Spain
F.I.S.A. Palaudarias, 26 - 08004 Barcelona

*The Battle of St Quentin. Scenes of the Spanish troops departing from St Quentin (detail).*

*Battle of St Quentin (France) in 1557. The taking of Noyon.*

# THE FOUNDATION OF THE MONASTERY OF THE ESCORIAL

## The Battle of St Quentin, August 10 1557

On January 17 1556, Charles V signed the documents ceding Castille and Aragon with all their possessions to Prince Philip. To ensure a peaceful beginning to his son's reign, the Emperor concluded a five year treaty with Henry II of France, but the voluble French monarch made a simultaneous pact with the Pope which committed him to help with men and money in the event of a war with Spain: in return he was to receive the throne of Naples for his son.

War broke out in September and Philip II's army in the Low Countries, under the command of Manuel Filiberto, Duke of Savoy, composed of thirty-five thousand infantry, twelve thousand horse and plentiful artillery, marched on the important French city of St Quentin, which was surrounded in July 1557. The Constable of Montmorency tried to come to the aid of the city with a French army of eighteen thousand infantry and six thousand horse; on August 10, at the head of his men, he made a supreme effort. Of the two thousand men sent to the relief of the city, only four hundred entered St Quentin; the rest were scattered and killed by the Spanish. The Frenchman withdrew, considering that he had achieved his aim of relieving the besieged. Then the Duke of Savoy ordered the Count of Egmont, a general of cavalry, to

pursue Montmorency and keep him busy fighting until he came up with the main body of troops. Montmorency soon realised that he had no choice and, disposing his troops, fought bravely at the outset, but when the Spanish infantry and artillery came up, the French retreated, and the retreat became a chaotic rout, though the Gascon infantry fought valiantly until they were swept aside by cannon fire. The Constable of Montmorency, the Dukes of Montpensier and Longueville, the Prince of Mantua and more than 300 knights and 5,000 soldiers were made prisoner, only 600 knights and six thousand soldiers remaining in the field. The Spanish, who had about a thousand dead, seized all the enemy artillery, the munitions and baggage and eighty flags. On the following day, Philip II, in full armour, reviewed the troops and ordered the humble soldiers to be released and the knights to be kept in fortresses and castles. The siege of St Quentin continued and, in spite of the heroic defence put up by the besieged, the walls were breached in eleven places and Spanish, English, Flemish and German troops assaulted, entered and sacked the city on August 27. The war went on with various encounters which are of no interest to this story and Philip II, having signed the peace treaty at Câteau-Cambrésis on April 3 1559, returned to Spain, landing at Laredo on September 8 the same year.

Back in Spain, Philip II commanded a search for a suitable site to found a monastery to be dedicated to the glory of Saint Lawrence, the Spanish martyr, in

fulfilment of the vow he had made during the siege of St Quentin and, at the same time, to carry out the task, bequeathed to him by his father the Emperor Charles V in his last codicile, of showing him a place where his bones and those of his descendents might rest in honour and dignity.

A committee of philosophers, architects and masons carefully examined various sites over a period of two years and chose a hill hard by the small town of El Escorial, which seemed the most appropriate place in view of the abundance and sweetness of the waters, the purity of the air and the plentiful supply of materials of all kinds for the work they would undertake in the surrounding area.

When the new foundation had been proposed to the Order of St Jerome and duly accepted, the nearby town of Guadarrama, on November 30 1561, became the meeting place of Juan Bautista de Toledo, the King's chief architect, Pedro de Hoyo, secretary to Philip II, Fray Juan de Huete and Fray Juan de Colmenar, Hieronymite monks, future Prior and Vicar of the new Monastery, both well versed in architecture, and other monks. When they had seen and approved the chosen site, they all returned to Madrid.

In April and May 1562, the dense clumps of rockrose which clung to the ground were torn up, the lime ovens were made, the site was marked out by Juan Bautista de Toledo in the presence of Philip II and the inspector, the accountant and the clerk of the new works arrived.

At the beginning of July came the Hieronymite who was to be the soul of the enterprise: Fray Antonio de

*Construction of the Monastery after a drawing of 1576 by an unknown author.*

*View of the Royal Monastery of San Lorenzo. 17th century Spanish school.*

Villacastín, lay chorister, the most distinguished builder of the Order of St Jerome in Spain and right hand, from that time on, of the architects Juan Bautista de Toledo and Juan de Herrera.

The preliminaries were completed and the first stone laid on April 23 1563. The hand of Juan de Herrera wrote on the sides three Latin inscriptions referring to the act. When the stone had been blessed, Juan Bautista de Toledo, Andrés de Almaguer and other officials and some Hieronymites set it in place. Although he was present, Fray Antonio de Villacastín did not wish to help them to lay it; he said that he would save himself for the last stone, as indeed was the case. It was eleven in the morning. They all returned to have lunch in the town of El Escorial.

Five year from the start, the Site suffered a severe blow: Juan Bautista de Toledo, distinguished architect, designer and mathematician, died in Madrid on May 21 1567. His successor was Juan de Herrera, who had assisted him on the project since the beginning.

On the Day of the Innocents in the same year, 1567, in the presence of Philip II, the first six sons of the Monastery took their vows. They were: Fray Juan del Espinar, once a votary at Guadalupe and now procurator of San Lorenzo; Fray Juan de San Jerónimo, votary at Salamanca, preacher and delegate; Fray Juan de San Jerónimo, votary at Guisando, keeper of the chest and author of the History of the foundation of the house; Fray Francisco de Cuéllar, a votary from Almedilla, in charge of the quarries; Fray Antonio de Villacastín, a votary of the Sisla in Toledo, lay

5

*Romantic view of the Monastery. Van Hale (signed 1851).*

chorister, chief worker at the Factory and high in the esteem of Philip II; and Fray Alonso del Escorial, cook and nurse to the poor.

The Site grew rapidly and in June 1571 the monks could already take up residence in San Lorenzo, leaving the house in El Escorial which they had lived in until then; it was later converted into a hospital.

At three in the afternoon on June 7 1573, the bodies of Queen Isabel of Valois and Prince Charles were brought to the Monastery with a great train of monks and courtiers in mourning.

On Febraury 4 the next year the bodies of the Emperor Charles V, the Empress Isabel, the Princess María, Philip II's first wife, Eleanor, Queen of France and of various Princes and Princesses arrived and were placed beneath the altar of the old church.

The foundations of the main church were laid while Philip II was in San Lorenzo on June 14 1575. In the same month the Library was delivered: it consisted of 4,000 selected volumes, printed or in manuscript, mostly taken from the King's own collection.

At this time there was a wide variety of divergent opinions among the Congregation at the Site. Herrera proposed that the stone should be brought already cut and carved from the quarries, as distinct from the system used up to that time. He met with the opposition of almost all the other directors of the works, but when the King had visited the quarries in person and weighed up the expense and inconvenience of continuing to carve the stone next to the Site or doing it at the quarries, Philip himself commanded that Herrera's proposal be adopted.

*Panorama of the Monastery from the "Horizontal" walk.*

*Fantastic panorama of the Monastery. David Roberts (1796-1864). Engraved by Frectairn and published in 1836.*

In the summer of the same year Don John of Austria, beloved of the Hieronymites, spent several days in the Monastery. On September 8 the Royal Family — except the King, who did not attend —, were regaled with a bullfight and the convent invited their royal guests to a meal at which the following fare was served: «A salad with diverse sauces. Six melons. Four roasted capons. Two omelettes with fried bacon and livers. Eight seasoned fowl. Four geese in breadcrumbs. Two cured legs of ram. Two large dished of quinces. Two more large dishes of pears. Two more dishes of pippins. Two dishes of jam. Half a dozen sauce boats of jelly with doughnuts. Three ham hocks. Two cows' tongues. All of this — adds the historian, who was present at the feast —, was gar-

nished and done to a turn and served with great solemnity.»

On November 9 in the following year 1576, Bautista de Cabrera, on the orders of Philip II, left for El Pardo with fifty men who bore back on their shoulders a marble Crucifix by Benvenuto Cellini.

At the end of March and the beginning of April in 1577 Philip was in San Lorenzo to celebrate Easter and he performed the Maundy ceremony, washing the feet of ten poor people and serving them at table assisted by his nephews Albert and Wenceslas, Archdukes of Austria.

On May 24 1579, a Sunday, at seven in the evening, Busto de Villegas, Bishop of Avila and the Maestre de Campo Don Gabriel Niño, brought the body of Don

*East façade from the garden.*

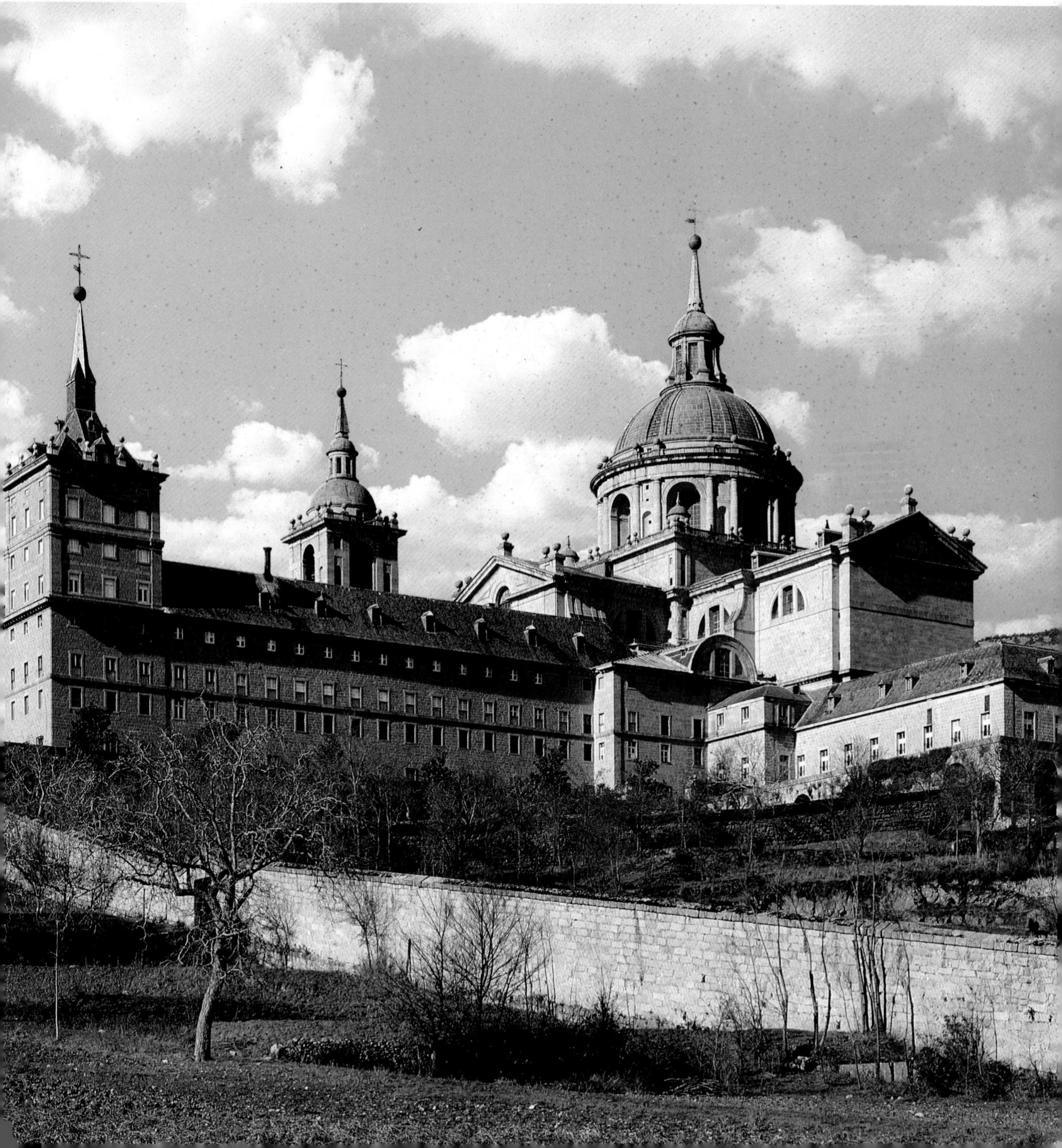

*South façade.*

John of Austria, son of the Emperor Charles V.

In the summer of 1580 Spain was scourged and devastated by a pestilential catarrh (influenza); all the monks of San Lorenzo fell sick and three friars died besides Fray Andrés de León, a famous book illuminator.

In the midst of the officials, pieceworkers and workers on the Site, armed with their instruments of office, Philip II was solemnly received on March 24 1583 at eleven in the morning. He was returning from Portugal, having achieved the union of that Crown with the Crown of Castile.

On July 30 and during the first days of August 1584, the colossal stone kings, which weigh about twenty-five tons and now adorn the Kings' Courtyard, to which they have given their name, were raised into place. They were dragged from the quarry by forty pairs of oxen. They are the work of the Toledan sculptor Juan Bautista Monegro, who was paid twelve thousand ducats for his work.

On September 13 the last stone was laid in the presence of Philip II and his children, Fray Juan de San Jerónimo, and Fray Antonio de Villacastín, who had seen the first one laid twenty-one years before. Villacastín gives the news in his History: «In thirteen days in September 1584, the last stone of this building of San Lorenzo the Royal was laid; it was on a cornice on the wall of the portico, on the left side going into the courtyard; a black cross was made on the fillet, and on the underside a box was made and a parchment placed inside with the day and year, the Gospels and other holy things, and who was the King and the Pope and the Prior of this House and other things worthy of record». The main church was inaugurated with a solemn procession to carry the Holy Sacrament on August 9, 1586. The poles of the canopy were borne by Philip II, Prince Philip and knights of the household; on the following day, the feast of St Lawrence, after the procession through the church attended by His Majesty and the court, mass was sung in the Royal Chapel and the Prior del Parral, Fray José de Sigüenza, preached a fine sermon.

Now that the church was finished, the King commanded that all the bodies of the Royal Family, which had until then been in temporary resting places in the church, be placed beneath the high altar of the main church and on November 3, 4 and 5, eighteen bodies were carried on the shoulders of the monks to their new grave.

*The Monastery from the Batán dam.*

*South façade of the Monastery, Convalescents' Gallery, pool and garden.*

# THE ESCORIAL: ITS ARCHITECTURE

## The exterior of the building

Two great squares flank the building on the north and west; the west square is 52 metres wide and the north square 36. They are bounded by a finely carved wall of granite, adorned with pilasters and balls, and the nine entrances are closed by strong iron chains. Around the Colonnades are the Household Staff Quarters, Ministries, Houses of the Infantes and the Queen, and the Company, all built of granite in harmony with the style of the Monastery.

An underground passage crosses the Colonnade on the north side from the Staff Quarters to the entrance hall of the Palace. It was built in the time of Charles III to cross the Colonnade without having to brave the lashing winds which blow on winter days. The Company House is connected to the Monastery by a passageway — which encloses the Colonnade on the west side — paved in slate and adorned with pilasters, windows and arches.

On the east and south sides the Colonnades are replaced by elegant gardens 27 metres wide on an embankment raised on 77 stonework arches almost 8 metres high, which is more than 543 metres long. Between the stone wall of the embankment and the building are the superb hanging gardens: they well deserve the name, since they are on vaults resting on pilasters, forming tasteful nooks, niches and seats which can be reached down 12 flights of steps. There are twelve fountains in the garden and around them squares of box hedge which are a delight to the eye.

## The façades

The main façade faces west. It is 207 metres long and 20 high with two 55 metre high towers at the ends terminating in slate covered pyramids finished with a ball 1.38 metres in diameter made of bell metal, with weather vane and cross at the apex. A cornice runs all around the building at a height of 17 metres. The lower or main body, in Doric style, rests on a dado about one metre high.

On the west façade is the main entrance to the Monastery, 3 metres wide and 6 high. A window opens above the door and at the sides are grids in relief. The sides of the door are adorned by four half columns with niches and windows. The first storey of the main doorway is finished with an architrave, a frieze and a cornice supported by capitals.

The second body, which is Ionic, rests on the cornice of the first and has only four half columns. In a niche in the central space is a 4 metre high statue of St Lawrence made of granite, with hands and head of white marble, the work of the Toledan sculptor and architect Juan Bautista Monegro; and below the saint, a shield with the royal coat of arms, carved by the same artist. The portico is rounded off by a triangular frontispiece with acroterions and balls.

*North and west façades.*

The south façade is the most beautiful of all. It is 161 metres long and a 5 metre buttress rises from the embankment gardens to the level of the Colonnade. This façade has 296 windows.

The east façade is the first to greet the visitor walking up from the station. A smooth frontispiece, with no windows or decoration, rises in the centre and forms the rear of the main chapel. At the ends of the façade are two towers and there are 386 windows on five levels.

The main entrance is on the west façade and gives onto a spacious hall 8 metres wide by 23 long, with two doors on the sides and windows above them. The vault is stone and projecting pilasters and arches are to be seen on the walls.

*Garden of Philip II's Summer Palace.*

*The Friars' Garden at the foot of the south façade.* ▷

# The King's Courtyard

This takes its name from the six 5 metre high statues of Kings of Judea which adorn the façade of the Church. The courtyard is 64 metres long and 38 wide and has windows on four levels: 80 on each side. Counting those of the towers and the dormer windows in the slate roofs, the grand total is 276. On the left or right wall, according to how one enters, between the eighth and ninth windows, is the last stone to be placed in the building, marked with a small black cross echoed on the roof by another larger cross formed by the cut of the slates.

Juan Bautista Monegro made these statues of the kings from a single slab of granite, except for the heads, feet and hands, which are made of white mar-

*The Kings' Courtyard.*

*Detail of the exterior of the Basilica Choir.*

ble. The sceptres, crowns and insignias, of gilded bronze, were carved by the sculptor Sebastián Fernández.

The kings and the inscriptions which can be seen on the pedestals on which they rest are the following:

*David:* Operis exemplan a Domino recepit (He received from the Lord the model of the Temple).

*Solomon:* Templum Domino aedificatum dedicavit (He dedicated to the Lord the Temple he built for Him).

*Hezekiah:* Mundata domo phase celebravit (Having restored and cleaned the Temple, he celebrated the Passover).

*Josiah:* Volumen Legis Domini instauravit (He found the Volume of the Law of the Lord).

*Jehosophat:* Lucis ablatis Legem propagavit (Having destroyed the idolatrous woods, he spread the Law).

*Manasseh:* Contritus altare Domini instauravit (Having repented, he restored the altar of the Lord).

The blackened bronze inscriptions are written on great slabs of white marble, which clash strongly with the dark grey of the granite. These inscriptions or legends are an admirable summary, made by Fray Francisco de los Santos, of the ones conceived for the same purpose by Father Sigüenza, which were never installed. The present ones were put in place in 1660.

*Portico of the Basilica.*

## The façade of the Church

The Church rises at the end of the Kings' Courtyard on a broad platform which is reached by seven steps occupying the full width of the courtyard. It is in the Doric style and consists of two bodies with two towers at the sides.

The first body is formed by six columns and five arches 3.90 metres wide and 8 metres high. Above each arch there is a balcony with iron railings and about 16 metres from the ground runs a cornice supporting the pedestals of the statues of the Israelite kings.

The second body, which rises from this cornice, is composed of six great pedestals — resting directly on the half columns of the first body — with inscriptions alluding to the six kings and their names. Between the pedestals an iron balustrade runs all the way along the façade, and there are three windows above the balconies of the first body, ending with a broad frontispiece whose tympanum is cut in the middle by a great window which lights the Choir and Church. In the original plan, instead of the kings, there were to be six stone pyramids similar to those on the main façade.

## The towers

At the sides of the façade of the church, and partly incorporated into the building, are two stone towers which are not visible below a height of 22 metres, which means that they look lower and less graceful than they really are. These towers are 72 metres high in all and end in a pyramid shaped stone spire crowned by a bell metal ball 1.39 metres in diameter, rounded off with crosses and weather vanes.

In the left-hand tower there were two rings of bells which were burned in 1671 and 1826; in the right-hand one are the temple bells and clock.

*The Pharmacy Tower.*

*The College Tower.*

*Detail of the lantern of the dome in the transept of the Basilica.*

*View of the nave and transept, Gospel side.* ▷

## The interior of the building

It is 38 metres long and 5 wide and the vault rests on ten arches matching those of the entrance. All the arches in the church wall have their doors; the three central ones give onto the atrium of the church, or lower Choir.

The door frames are made of finest acana wood from the West Indies and the panelling is of oak. The central door fills the arch and the two side doors leave space, in the curve of the arch, for two black marble medallions with inscriptions in raised letters of gilded bronze which, translated into English, read as follows: «Philip, King of all the Spains, of the two Sicilies, of Jerusalem, etc., laid the first stone of this temple, dedicated to the martyr St Lawrence, on St Bernard's day in the year 1563. Divine office was first held here on the Eve of St Lawrence in the year 1586»; and «Philip II, King of all the Spains, of the two Sicilies, of Jerusalem, etc., filled with piety and devotion, had this basilica consecrated with the holy chrism by the hand of Camilo Cayetano, Patriarch of Alexandria, apostolic Nuncio, on August 30, 1595.»

## The Atrium of the Church or Lower Choir

This forms a square of 16.71 metres. It has four chapels and four fonts for holy water. Three arches, closed by gilded bronze railings, lead into the church. Two of the chapels are used as chancels, and the other two are dedicated to the holy martyrs Cosmas and Damian and to St Sixtus and St Blaise. The vault is admired because, in spite of its length, it appears as smooth as the floor and even to be slightly convex.

*Atrium or Lower Choir. Detail.*

## The Church

From the seminary choirs a door leads to the temple; it is 3.62 metres wide and 7.24 high and the finely carved bronze grille was made and gilded in Zaragoza in Tujarón's workshop. The grilles of four other matching doors are made of the same material and by the same hand. The church forms a square with sides some 50 metres long, and the predominant architectural style is Doric in imitation of the design of St Peter's in Rome, according to the plan of the Italian engineer Francisco Paciotti, modified by Juan de Herrera. The vaults of the church rest on four enormous pillars, the supports of the gigantic cupola which rises 91 metres above the floor. On the sides of the pillars looking towards the minor naves, there are altars; in the upper one a gallery with a gilded bronze parapet and no means of access. Opposite these four central pillars, eight more emerge from the church walls — each with its altar and a gallery with access — about 30 centimetres from the wall. There are twenty-four arches around the church, forming three naves. Light floods into this grandiose basilica through 38 windows. The floor is of white and brown marble with simple patterns matching the severe majesty of the whole building. The total cost of the church was five and a half million reals in copper coin.

The vaults, made of brick coated on the outside with sheets of lead, were originally stuccoed on the inside with blue stars by Luca Cambiasso or *Luchetto* (except for the one above the high altar), but were fresco painted by Luca Giordano in the reign of Charles III.

*View of the nave and transept, Epistle side.*

*Overall view of the Choir.*

## MARBLES AND BRONZES

### The candelabras and lamp

Two huge, beautiful gilded bronze candelabras are kept in the church: the Carnation, made in Anvers in 1571 by Juan Simón; and the Tenebrae which, though it bears no inscription, is of the same style and manufacture as the other.

The lamp, which is used to light the Sacrament, is placed near the Chancel and, although there is nothing special about it, it cost 340,000 reals and the silk cord from which it hangs another 7,000. It is made of gilded bronze and is the work of the Madrid silversmiths Don Nicolás Cervantes and Don Manuel García, about 1883.

### The pulpits

They are on the first step up to the high altar and made of fine marble, with gilded bronze columns, rails and ornaments. The one on the right facing the altar has a gilded bronze medallion representing the four Doctors of the Church and the arms of the Monastery, and the one on the left another with the four Evangelists and the royal coat of arms. The delicately worked gilded sounding boards are supported by four slim columns and rounded off by statues of Faith and Religion. They were made by sawing the panels of a pulpit in Párraces and commissioned from Don Manuel de Urquiza by Ferdinand VII. They cost a million and a half reals. Nevertheless, their richness and exquisite workmanship clash with the overall austerity of the Basilica.

*The High Altar, from a design by Juan de Herrera.*

## The Chancel

This is a continuation of the central nave of the church, from which it is separated by twelve steps made of blood red marble from Espeja (Soria). It is 19 metres long and 14 wide. At the top of the steps is the Presbytery, with its floor of white, green and red marble and jasper, exquisitely and artfully inlayed. Up a further five steps is a platform decorated with gilded bronze rails. In the centre of this second platform, at the top of two stairs, stands the high altar, fashioned from a beautiful combination of marble and jasper and set apart from the rest; it is 3.50 metres long and 1.25 metres deep. The altarstone is a single piece of fine jasper covering the whole altar. At the sides — against the walls — there are two seats of fine wood with back rests.

## The reredos

This is made of jasper, marble and gilded bronze and is 14 metres wide by 26 high.
On the second level of the Chancel there is a dado 2,76 metres high with frieze and cornice running the full width of the Chancel; it is made of blood red marble with parts of Sierra Nevada serpentine.
On the right and left sides of this socle two splendid mahogany doors, plated on the temple side with the finest jasper in a variety of gorgeous colours, with frames and mouldings of gilded bronze, lead to the Shrine. The four registers, or horizontal zones, of the reredos rest on this socle.
The first is Doric with six almond marble columns 70 centimetres in diameter and 5 metres high. The centre is occupied by the Tabernacle, made by Giacomo Trezzo. A the sides, in green jasper niches, are gilded bronze statues of St Jerome and St Augustine. St Ambrose and St Gregory, the work of Leone and Pompeo Leoni, and two oil paintings: *The Adoration*

*St Matthew by Leone and Pompeo Leoni.*

*St Augustine by Leone and Pompeo Leoni (1509-1590 and 1533-1608).*

of the Shepherds and *The Adoration of the Kings* by Peregrine de Peregrini, or Pellegrini, Tibaldi.

The second register, Ionic, also has larger than life size gilded bronze statues of the four Evangelists the work of Leone and Pompeo Leoni, and three paintings: in the centre, *The Martyrdom of St Lawrence* by Peregrine de Peregrini, Tibaldi; and on the sides, *The Flagellation of the Saviour* and *Christ carrying the Cross* by Federico Zúccaro.

The third register, Corinthian, has four columns and two statues of the same material, the work of the same craftsmen, which show St Andrew and St James the Greater, Apostles, and three paintings by Zúccaro: *The Assumption of the Virgin, The Resurrection of Christ* and *The Descent of the Holy Ghost.*

On the fourth and last register there is a chapel with a magnificent Crucifix, images of the Virgin and St John and of St Peter and St Paul, the work of Pompeo Leoni, all of gilded bronze.

The reredos cost, 3,803,825 reals and 12 maravedis.

*Calvary by Leone and Pompeo Leoni.*

*The Martyrdom of St Lawrence by Peregrino di Peregrini, «Il Tibaldi», (1527-1596).*

*The Adoration of the Kings by Peregrini.*

*The Adoration of the Shepherds by Peregrini.*

FEDERICII ZVCCARVS
I · S · 87 ·

The
Assumption
of the Virgin
by Federico
Zúccaro
(1542-1609).

*Christ bearing the Cross by Zúccaro.*

*The Flagellation by Zúccaro.*

*Philip II and group at prayer and the Tabernacle.*

## The Shrine and the Tabernacle

The Shrine is an arch 1.38 metres deep opening behind the centre of the first register of the reredos; two marble staircases lead up to it. These have eleven steps and two landings; the upper one leads to the Tabernacle. The walls are of red marble with white inlays, and from the last landing to the curve of the arch (which looks like a rainbow) the fresco represents: *The Sacrifice to Melchizedek, The Israelites gathering manna, The Legal Supper* and *Elijah receiving the bread baked under ashes,* all works by Tibaldi.

The Tabernacle is one of the gems of the world and possibly the finest work of its kind in existence. It is situated in the arch formed between the centre columns of the first register of the altar. It is round and in the Corinthian style, made of the finest marbles and jaspers and gilded bronze. On a jasper socle, eight columns of red jasper veined with white from Aracena (Huelva), of a singular beauty and so hard that they had to be shaped with diamonds, support a cornice with its corbels, rosettes and other decorations. These columns are surrounded by a cylindrical body with mouldings, niches and doors. At the four cardinal points four doors are represented: two open and protected by glass panes and two closed. On the cornice runs a podium with eight pedestals which finish the columns below and act as platforms for gilded bronze figures of the Apostles, 27.862 centimetres high which, with four more statuettes in the niches between the columns of the first register, make up the full complement of the Apostolate. Dismantled by the French, it was restored by Don Manuel de Urquiza at the orders of Ferdinand VII, as the following inscription says: Penetrale Jesv Christo sacrvm Gallorvm aggresione dirvtvm Ferdinandvs VII Rex Pivs. Avg. restitvit MDCCXXVII — which, translated into English, means: "Shrine dedicated to Jesus Christ, destroyed during an attack by the French. Ferdinand VII, august and pious King, restored it, 1827." The magnificent monstrance inside, of purest gold, adorned and embellished with precious stones and a topaz as large as a fist hanging from the rosette of the Tabernacle, disappeared during the Napoleonic invasion.

On the lower socle of the Tabernacle, between two columns, is a Latin inscription by Arias Montano — Iesvcristo Sacerdoti ac Victimae Philipvs II, Rez. D. Opvs. Iacobi Treci mediolanens, totvm hispano e lapide — which, being translated, means: "To Jesus Christ, priest and victim, Philip II, king, dedicated this work, all of Spanish marble, made by Giacomo Trezzo of Milan".

Monument
of the
Emperor
Charles V.

## The Royal Monuments

The royal monuments, in the Doric style, are situated in two large arches opening off the sides of the Chancel. On the first landing of the altar a dado, 3 metres high, runs across the full 8 metre width of the arch; in it are three doors with jambs and lintels made of Sierra Nevada serpentine, with gilded bronze decoration and frames. A chapel, 2,78 metres deep, running the full width of the arch, is formed on the dado. The outer columns and pilasters are matched by others within, whose spaces and sides are covered with black marble and adorned with inscriptions in gilded bronze raised lettering. In the central spaces on both sides are five larger than life size statues of figures in prayer, made of gilded bronze, copper and brass.

On the Gospel side the first and main figure is that of the Emperor Charles V, armed and wearing the imperial robe, on which a two-headed eagle is inlaid in fine stone the colour of the bird itself. On his right is the Empress Isabel, mother of Philip II; behind, his daughter Princess Maria, also with the robe and imperial eagle; and then Princess Eleanor and Princess Maria, the Emperor's sisters, all kneeling with their hands joined in prayer.

Philip II was so anxious to see them that he had them modelled in plaster and gilded by Nicolás Granello and his brother Fabrizio Castello (the latter also painted some of the coats of arms in oils for the funerals) and painted like the real ones — they remained there as substitutes until the real ones were finally set in place: the figure of Charles V in 1597 and that of Philip II in 1600.

On the opposite wall is an epitaph in Latin which in English says: "To the honour and glory of Almighty God. To Charles V, August Emperor, King of these lands, of Sicily and Jerusalem, Archduke of Austria, and to his good father, dedicated by his son Philip II. Here also lie Isabel, his wife and Maria, his daughter, Empresses; Eleanor and Maria, his sisters, Queens: the first of France, the second of Hungary."

The statues of the other monuments, on the Epistle side, match the ones opposite. The first is of Philip II, dressed in the robe with the royal arms and his head uncovered. On his right, Queen Anne, his fourth and last wife and mother of Philip III; behind, Queen Isabel of Valois, his third wife; on her right, Princess Maria of Portugal, his first wife and mother of Prince Charles; and the Prince behind his mother.

The inscriptions on this monument read in English: "To Almighty God, Philip II, Catholic King: of all the kingdoms of Spain, of Sicily and Jerusalem, Archduke of Austria, when still living, commanded them to be placed in the this holy temple which he raised from its foundations. Beside him rest Ana Isabel and Maria, his wives, and Prince Charles his first born son".

*Monument
of King
Philip II.*

*Detail of Room V of the Art Gallery, dedicated to Ribera.*

# PAINTINGS IN THE ESCORIAL

At all times, but especially in the 16th Century, no palace, church or building of any importance could be conceived without paintings. Philip II and his collaborators on the Escorial gradually planned the various pictures which would decorate the Monastery.

According to a minutely detailed plan, painting would be incorporated into the building: the murals to be painted in fresco and easel paintings done specially for the Monastery. To these must be added those sent by the King to be hung in certain places. All of them would be part of the iconography planned not only for the Basilica, but also for the different places where the images of the saints were to arouse and foment the devotion and piety of the monks, such as the cells, the Refectory, the Library and even the cloisters where they walked.

Another part of the Monastery was also filled with paintings, but without a preconceived plan: the royal apartments, where a host of devotional paintings, family portraits and profane canvasses were hung, since Philip II was a lover of all of them. This interest in painting came from his great-grandparents, the Catholic Kings, especially Isabella, who had put together an extraordinary collection of great works of art, but in particular works by Flemish painters. She began the custom of the Court Painter who, from that time on, would be part of the household of all the kings of Spain. The great Queen's own painter was John of Flanders, who has left us a portrait of her (now in the Pardo Palace in Madrid).

Philip II, like his father, was a great patron of art. The great Italian masters of the day worked for him. There is a famous anecdote which tells how the Emperor Charles V was visiting Titian's studio and watching him painting. When the master dropped a brush, he immediately bent and picked it up for him, to the astonishment of all those present and the embarrassment of the painter himself. Many letters were exchanged between Philip II and the old painter in which we can see that the son fully shared the regard and admiration felt by his father, the Emperor. The artist, for his part, felt great respect and veneration for the King, and Philip's wish was his command. This admiration of the King for the great foreign masters in no way lessened the protection and help which he extended to the outstanding artists of Spain. For this reason, in the 16th Century the Kings of Spain possessed the finest collection of painting of any Court in Europe.

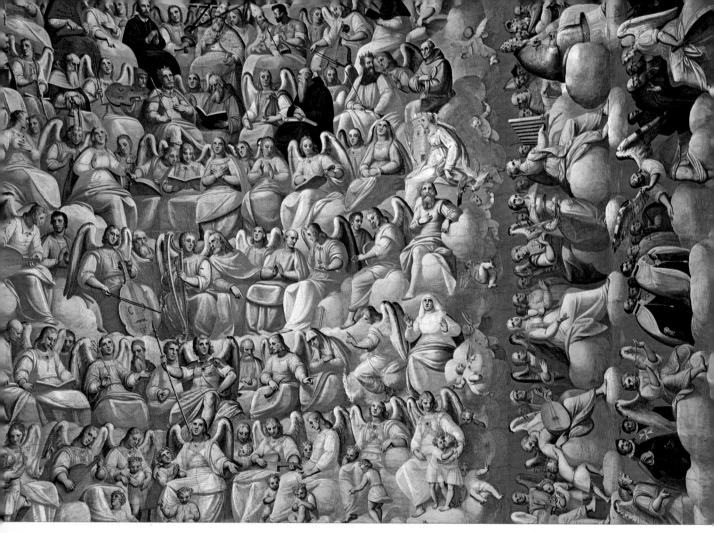

*The Glory, fresco painting on the vault of the Choir by
Luca Cambiaso, «Il Luchetto», (1527-1585).*

## Mural paintings

When the moment came to find the artists for the work, the King looked towards nearby Italy. This choice was probably influenced by the advice of Juan Bautista de Toledo, the architect who, as we know, worked there, but undoubtedly the main reason was that there were no Spanish painters of the necessary quality at that time. Gaspar Becerra, who had worked in Italy with Michaelangelo, was dead. On his return to Spain, he entered Philip II's service in 1562, worked on the decoration of the Alcazar in Madrid, the Pardo Palace and the Descalzas Reales, but died very young and his only surviving fresco is a ceiling in the Pardo Palace (all the rest have been destroyed by fire). The

King thought of bringing Titian's finest disciple, Veronese, to decorate the ceilings, but he refused in spite of the extraordinary conditions he was offered, doubtless because the great ceiling decorations of the Palace of the Doges of Venice are not fresco painted but done on canvasses which were later stuck to the ceiling.

The ambassadors looked for other painters of renown but, unfortunately, the artists contracted were second rate and pleased neither the King nor the friars. This was why more than a century passed, as we shall see, before the mural paintings were successfully completed.

The first of the fresco painters to work at the Escorial was Nicola Granello. This painter had come from Italy

*Detail of the Choir. The great organ and Cambiasso's vault.*

*Detail of the vault and frieze on the weast side. Frescoes by Luca Giordano.*

with his step-father Gianbattista Castello, called the Bergamasque (since he was from Bergamo), a painter and architect who worked on the Alcazar Real in Madrid. With him was his brother Fabrizio Castello and other lesser painters, Lagaro Tavaron, Francisco de Urbino and Orazio Cambiasso. Their first work was the Choir of the Basilica, which was to be decorated with coffers which disappeared later when the Gloria was painted, just as it is today. Then they decorated the vaults of the Chapterhouses, the Lower Prior's Cell and the Battle Gallery. They followed the style of Rafael in the decoration of the Loggia at the Vatican. They reproduce the ''grotesque'' of Nero's Domus Aurea, a combination of floral motifs and trophies of war, all with highly geometrical structures.

In the painting of these ceilings, the two brothers did not show an outstanding talent for composition, but they did leave a fresco of considerable iconographic rather than pictorial interest. This is the *Battle of Higueruela,* a small place near Granada, conquered in the 14th century by King John II of Castile. In the Alcazar in Segovia there were some black and white drawings by an unknown author depicting this battle. Philip II wanted a copy to be made in a great hall which would run the full length of the north gallery of the Basilica. It begins with a depiction of the Christian encampment and then shows the marchpast of the army. In the foreground is Don Alvaro de Luna, John II's Favourite, with the whole household and their ensigns and banners unfurled; then, the King, in the

midst of his court and his standards, both retinues on horseback; then comes the encounter of the two armies — the Moorish and the Christian — and, finally, the walled town of Higueruela and the Christians seizing it. The great interest of the painting lies in the fact that the author of the drawings lived at the time of the battle. It is an incomparable graphic document which shows the armour, the weapons and the attire of the time. The standards borne by the different army corps tell us which troops and which gentlemen from different European kingdoms took part in the battle. The composition is full of life and movement, making the fresco fascinating to look at. On the opposite wall, on the canvasses between the balconies, the Battle of St Quentin was painted. Here too we can see the various

phases: the King's encampment, the march-past of the army, the site of the Town and the Battle. Nevertheless, it lacks the vivacity and grace of the Higueruela painting, which leads one to think that the early drawings found in the Alcazar in Segovia were the work of a fine artist, who well deserved to have his work copied.

At the two ends of the gallery are *The Expedition to the Third Islands, or Azores,* painted in the time of Philip II. This is another valuable iconographic document, which shows the various ships in use at the time.

Luca Cambiasso, usually called "Luchetto", was accepted as the King's painter on November 19, 1583. He was a native of Moneglia near Genoa. A tremen-

*The resurrection of the dead for the Last Judgement by Giordano (1636-1705).*

dous reputation preceded him; one Italian painter swore that he had painted more frescoes than twelve painters could paint in their whole lives. It is said that he painted without making cartoons and sometimes used both hands. He was certainly a fast worker, since in less than a year he painted the vault of the Choir and on its walls *The Annunciation, The Four Theological Virtues, St Jerome* and *St Lawrence,* all larger than life size.

On the vault he depicted *The Glory.* In the centre, the Holy Trinity and, in symmetrical rows, the Cherubim and the Choirs of Angels according to their rank. It was criticised from the beginning, since it lacks grace and composition. Although the drawing is correct, the figures are rigid and there is no subtlety in the shadows or depth in the grounds. Moreover, the colours are lifeless and uninspiring.

This was attributed by some to the fact Luchetto had to bow to the rules laid down by the theologians, but this has no foundation. Undoubtedly he had to paint *The Glory* there according to the plan, but the creation of the scene was up to him. Other writers have attributed this failure to the crisis in the painter's love life which arose when he was unable to marry the woman he loved, but this also seems very unlikely. On the right of the vault he painted his own portrait together with Father Villacastín.

The other fresco by him is in the Main Chapel, where he painted *The Crowning of Mary* and the four major prophets on the lunettes. Here the composition is less

*The Glory on the vault of the great staircase of the Monastery by Giordano.*

*The Battle of La Higueruela in 1431. Skirmishes between
Castilian and Granadan troops.*

stiff than in the Choir and the colours are fresher, but
even here he can hardly be considered a master of
colour or composition.

In 1586 a new painter came to Spain from Italy:
Peregrine, known as Tibaldi after his father Tibaldo.
He as born in Puria and trained as a painter in
Bologna. He wa a Mannerist decorator and follower
of Michaelangelo and had done major works when he
arrived in Spain — the vault of St Louis of France in
Rome, various palaces and churches in Bologna —
and, like Michaelangelo, he was a great architect. In
El Escorial he painted the dome of the Library and
decorated the Lower Cloister, undoubtedly the finest
frescoes of the first phase of the Monastery.

On the vault of the Library he showed that he was a
perfect decorator, an excellent composer, a great
draftsman and brilliant colourist.

Tibaldi's other paintings, the scenes in the Lower
Cloister, are a catchecism on the life of Jesus. This is
the cloister surrounding the Evangelists' Courtyard,
which begins on the north gallery with the *Embrace of
St Joachim and St Ann at the Golden Gate* and com-
pletes the full circuit of the arches with the scene of
the Last Judgement. This monumental work, with its
delightful composition, shows the influence of
Michaelangelo; nevertheless, the work fails in the col-
ouring, which is rather sour and at times even unplea-
sant. In the final scenes, Tibaldi's hand is less evident;
it is certain that only the drawing is his work and the
rest was done almost entirely by his assistants, the

Castello brothers, Urbina and Orazio Cambiasso.

The frescoes of the Shrine are also the work of Tibaldi, but it is impossible to visit them. It is a narrow space behind the High Altar which opens onto the Tabernacle. The themes all allude to the Sacrament, and the figures are smaller than life-size: *The Israelites collecting the Manna, the Supper of the Lamb, Abraham offering the tithe to Melchizedek,* and *Elijah receiving the bread baked under ashes from the Angel.* On the small vault, he painted the rainbow with angels' heads. It is executed with great care and attention, correct draftsmanship and good composition.

Tibaldi also painted, as we shall see, various easel works and, well paid and ennobled with the title Marquis of Milan, he returned to Italy.

After these fresco decorations were finished, almost two centuries would pass until all those planned were completed.

Not until 1692, in the reign of Charles II, was the decoration of the remaining vaults undertaken.

Father Francisco de los Santos, one of the historians

*The Battle of La Higueruela. The army of the Christian troops in battle order.*

*Episodes from the story of David by Giordano.*

of El Escorial, considers Charles II one of the great patrons of the Monastery. On June 7 1671, a terrible fire, which raged for more than a fortnight, destroyed a large part of the roofing in the monks' quarters. The King, who numbered among his virtues (of which little is usually said) taste and concern for the Fine Arts, immediately ordered the rebuilding of everything destroyed by the fire and set to work. Subsequently he undertook the most ambitious task to be attempted since the completion of the Monastery — the decoration of the vaults.

The concept of mural decoration had undergone a drastic change since the earlier frescoes had been painted. In Italy the Baroque was at its height and a Neapolitan painter, Luca Giordano, considered the finest fresco painter in Europe, held absolute sway. He was born about 1628; the exact date is not known. The son of a painter, he had grown up surrounded by brushes which, with his natural talent for art, made him one of the most consummate masters of his time and one of the most meteoric of any time. He was influenced by a great Spanish painter who lived in Naples, José Ribera. Later he went to Rome, where he learnt the technique of fresco with Pedro de Cortona, whom he surpassed in some ways.

A great draftsman, as can be seen from his daring use of foreshortening, he was gifted with an extraordinary facility for composition, which endows his canvasses with unusual movement and grandiosity. To all this he added a luminous palette, which made his ceilings the apotheosis of animation and colour. When he came to Spain preceded by a well-earned reputation, he was already a rich man. Here the King paid him munificently and heaped honours on him. He was said to be rather a pest, who contrived to secure important jobs for all his sons-in-law. The King was enthralled with his work and loved to watch him paint. Besides the frescoes, he left a collection of about fifty easel paintings which have been conserved by the various Palaces and Trusts.

There is a fund of stories about the dealings between the King and the painter, one of which refers to the great facility which Giordano had for imitating the style and manner of any painter, so that, when Charles II once complained that he had no twin to a work by Bassano, the artist painted him one in a few days, which was indistinguishable from an original. On another occasion Charles II's wife, Marianne of Neuburg, asked him why his wife remained in Naples. The painter dashed off a portrait of her to introduce

*Triumph of the Church Militant by Giordano.*

*The Gymnosophists on the frieze in the Library by Peregrini.*

her to the Queen, who was so amazed that she took off her pearl necklace and gave it to him as gift for his wife.

In May 1692 he arrived, accompanied by one of his sons and various helpers, and started work. In the summer of 1694 he returned to the Court, his work at the Escorial finished.

He began by painting the vault of the main staircase. In the centre the Holy Trinity bursts forth from a great break in the clouds. Next to the Son is the figure of Mary and a group of Angels supporting the Cross. On a lower level is the martyr St Lawrence offering the great work and interceding for the Kings of Spain. On the right, Charles V kneels and offers his two crowns and behind, Philip II offers a globe symbolising the Spanish Empire. Groups of Angels playing music, painted with a daring use of foreshortening, frame the central scene. From a balcony, Charles II contemplates the scene with his wife, Marianne of Neuburg and his mother, Marianne of Habsburg. There is no doubt that is one of the most outstanding frescoes in Europe. The perfect draftsmanship and the incomparably daring movement are matched by luminous, brilliant colour, which never becomes strident. These colours are characteristic of Giordano: pastel blues and greens, an occasional touch of crimson which, as they blend into the profusion of pinks of the flesh tones and the yellowish whites of the clouds, produce a dazzling splash of colour. He began the painting in September 1692 and finished in April 1693, a new record.

The King then wanted to continue with the vaults of the Church, of which Luchetto had painted only the Chancel and the Choir; eight were still to be done, and he lost no time in setting to work. The subjects depicted, beginning on the left facing the High Altar in the side nave, are the following: *The Mystery of the Incarnation, The Israelites crossing the Desert and the Red Sea* and *The Triumph of the Church Militant.* In the central nave, next to the Choir, *The Last Jugdement* and *The Resurrection of the Flesh.* Passing into the right-hand nave, *The Purity of the Holy Virgin, The Victory of the Israelites over the Amalekites, The Judgement of St Jerome* and *The Doctors of the Church.* The eighth, in the central nave next to the Chancel, is *The Death and Burial of the Holy Virgin.*

All bear witness to Giordano's extraordinary qualities as a fresco painter, as a composer, draftsman and colourist, but worth special mention are *The Triumph of the Church, The Judgement of St Jerome* and the *Death of the Virgin.* A preliminary sketch of this last work has been preserved in the Library of the Royal Palace in Madrid.

All this impressive work was carried out in sixteen months, between April 1693 and July 1694 and we can see Giordano's extraordinary qualities as a painter. He painted so fast not because he did it carelessly or lightly, but because he was a tireless worker; and, aware of the great task he had in hand, he prepared preliminary drawings and then the rough sketches or cartoons that he sent to the King. We know that he sent five such sketches of the vault depicting *The Triumph of the Church* to the King. He painted the composition on the vault, which had been prepared for the colours, and then, as a good fresco painter, he worked rapidly, not using brooms as has been rather contemptuously suggested, but with huge brushes made from vegetable material. Giordano's painting, as we can see, is extremely solid and well executed.

All the subjects of the vaults of the Escorial were not chosen arbitrarily by the painters, but were part of a perfectly conceived and studied plan, for great monuments always follow such a plan. In the case of Giordano's vaults, it must have been the Prior Fray Alonso de Talavera who studied and inspired the subjects; in any case, it was he who reported regularly to Charles II on the progress of the work.

*The God Pan by Peregrini, fresco on the Library ceiling.*

The Martyrdom of St James by Juan Fernández de Navarrete, «El Mudo», (1526-1579).

## Easel paintings

As we have already said, the easel paintings can be divided into three groups: those which were part of the iconographic plan of the Escorial, those which were brought there at the wish of its founder and those which all the Kings donated to the Monastery through the centuries.

Among the first group are the paintings of the minor retables and the High Altar. We mentioned all of them when we described the interior architecture of the Monastery; Spanish and Italian artists worked on them. Two Italians, Tibaldi and Zúccaro, worked on the High Reredos; the works of the latter practically disappeared during the repairs done by the Spanish painter Juan Gómez. On the other hand, the painters of the minor retables are Spanish. Navarrete, el Mudo (the Silent), who, in the opinion of Father Sigüenza, would have been the great painter of El Escorial and there would have been no need to summon Italians if death had not snatched him away so soon. Luis de Carvajal, a native of Toledo and disciple of Villodo, the imitator of Rafael, a fine draftsman and pleasant colourist. Miguel Barroso, also born in Toledo province in Consuegra, was a disciple of Gaspar Becerra, the architect, painter and sculptor, shows the strong influence of Michaelangelo inherited from his master. He painted the triptychs or altars of the Lower Cloister and did the drawings used by the embroiderers who worked in El Escorial on the liturgical robes, most of which have been conserved. All show religious scenes and refer to themes from the Gospels. Juan Gómez, who was mentioned when we spoke of Zúccaro, was another frequent worker in the Escorial. He collaborated with other painters, Zúccaro and Tibaldi, and worked alone on other pictures, such as the *Martyrdom of St Ursula.* Diego de Urbina is another of the painters of the minor retables. His place of birth is not known exactly, but we do know

*The Holy Family by Paolo Caliari, known as Veronese (1528?-1588).*

PĪS : DG : HIS
II · REX · ÆTA 66

*Philip II with the Golden Fleece by Alonso Sánchez Coello (1531-1588).*

55.

571.

*The Adoration of the Shepherds by Ribera, «El Españoleto», (1591-1652).*

that he was the son of another painter of the same name. It is noteworthy that most of the paintings done for the retables are dedicated to the female Saints. Last comes Sánchez Coello, Philip II's Household painter and his portraitist.

Many paintings by all the artists we have mentioned still exist; outstanding among them are those of Navarrete, who painted a *Holy Family, Jesus visiting his Mother after the Resurrection, The Nativity, Jesus being scourged at the pillar, The martyrdom of St James* and *The Burial of St Lawrence.*

An extraordinary number of paintings were collected in El Escorial. According to Poleró's catalogue, pro-

duced after the founding of The Prado Museum, the number reached about a thousand. Among the Spanish painters we have not mentioned, we should at least pick out those by Ribera, among which are: *The Holy Trinity, St Antony, The Nativity, The Entombment of Christ, St Peter in Prison, St Francis of Assisi, St Onofre* and *Jacob grazing Laban's sheep.* Velázquez is represented by *Joseph's Tunic.* El Greco's *St Maurice and the Theban Legionary* was painted for the Escorial, and other paintings were sent there: *St Peter, St Eugenius and St Francis,* of which two versions have been kept. Giordano is represented by: *Jael and Sisera, Jesus Served by the Angels, Job*

*Joseph's tunic by Velázquez (1599-1660). Detail.*

*Arachne and the Goddess Pallas by Giordano.*

*St Christopher with landscape by Joachim Patinir or Patenir (around 1480-1524).*

on the Dung Heap, The Calling of St Matthew, The Holy Family, a subject repeated on various occasions, and Balaam's Ass.

Apart from Giordano, the Neapolitan painter closely linked with Spain whom we have already spoken of, there are a large number of foreign artists. There are many works by Titian, Bosch and Coxcie. Works by the famous Venetian are: The Prayer in the Garden, The Martyrdom of St Lawrence and St Jerome at Prayer, all of which were painted specially for the Monastery; The Flight into Egypt, The Last Supper, Crucifix, which has hung in the Sacristy since its arrival, St John the Baptist, Madonna and Ecce Homo.

Many of Titian's works were moved to the Prado Museum, as were important works by Bosch, but the following have been preserved: The Haywain, The Road to Calvary, an Ecce Homo (The Insults) and a small panel of Paradise. Almost all the paintings by Michel Coxcie, which were presented by Philip II to the Monastery, have remained there; almost all are panels of considerable size: The Virgin with Child and several Saints, David cutting off Goliath's head, Mystic Subject, St Joachim presenting his offering in the Temple, St Joachim and St Ann with the Virgin and Child, the Martyrdom of St Philip.

Tintoretto has: The Adoration of the Shepherds,

*The Last Supper by Vecellio di Gregorio, «Titian»,*
*(1477?-1576).*

*David cutting off*
*Goliath's head by Michel*
*Coxcie (1499-1592).*

*Mystical marriage of St*
*Catherine and the Christ*
*Child, late 15th century*
*Dutch school.*

Part of Room II of the
Art Gallery, or Titian
Room.

The money changer and
his wife, signed in 1538
by Marinus Claesz van
Reymerswael (end of the
15th century-1567).

*The insults or Ecce Homo by Hieronymous Bosch (around 1460-1516).*

painted for the High Altar but never put there, *Jesus in the House of the Pharisee, The Conversion of Mary Magdalen, Queen Esther before Asuerus, The Entombment of Christ* and *Mystic Subject.* And Veronese: *The Adoration,* also destined for the High altar but never hung there, *The Eternal Father,* two *Descents, The Holy Family* and *Jesus appearing to this Mother after the Resurrection.*

We should also mention *St Christopher* by Patinir; *Virgin and Child by* Quentin Metsys; *The Last Judgement* by Peter Cocke and *The Presentation of the Virgin* by an unknown painter but, like the others, a Flemish panel.

Four still lifes by Mario Nuzzi, called Mario dei Fiori

because he painted still lifes with flowers, have been preserved; also various paintings by the Flemish flower painter Seghers.

We have only listed the first rank paintings, but many more hang in the cloisters, passages, cells and halls of the Monastery and Palace of El Escorial; some are originals and others ancient copies of the masters. To end this Chapter, let us mention the most important portraits conserved there: *The Founder,* by Antonio Moro; those by Sánchez Coello of *Princess Juana* and *Don John of Austria; Princess Marianne of Austria* and *Charles II* by Carreño de Miranda; and *Charles V* and *Philip II* by Pantoja de la Cruz.

*The descent from the Cross by Carlo Cagliari (1570-1596), on the altar in the Pantheon of the Infantes.*

## The altars of the Church

There are 44 altars or chapels including the High Altar. They have fine oil paintings with just a gilt frame and a simple arched frontispiece. The frontals are stucco and were made in 1829 by Don José Marzal, and the altar tables are of granite and rest on brown marble.

The altar paintings, beginning with the Gospel pulpit, are:

1. — St Peter and St Paul, painted by Juan Fernández Navarrete.

2. — Opposite: St Philip and St James, by the same painter. It was finished by Diego de Urbina.

3. — Altar of the Relics: The Annunciation, by Federico Zúccaro, restored by Juan Gómez.

4. — Chapel: St Ann, by Luca Cambiasso, Luchetto.

5. — Chapel: St John the Baptist Preaching in the Desert, by the same painter.

In the passageway of this chapel lies the body of Queen María de las Mercedes, first wife to Alfonso XII.

6. — St John the Evangelist and St Matthew, by Fernando Navarrete.

7. — Opposite: St Mark and St Luke, by the same painter.

8. — Chapel: St Ildefonsus and St Eugenius, archbishops of Toledo, by Diego de Urbina.

9. — Chapel: St Michael fighting the rebel angels, by Peregrine de Pergrini, Tibaldi.

10. — Chapel: St Isidore and St Leander, brothers, Achbishops of Seville, by Luis de Carvajal.

11. — St Fabian and St Sebastian, by Diego de Urbina.

12. — Opposite: The holy children Justus and Pastor, by Alonso Sánchez Coello.

13. — Chapel: The Martyrdom of St Maurice and the Theban Legionary, by Rómulo Cincinato.

*St Jerome at prayer. Portuguese reliquary, late 16th century.*

*Reliquary called «Milan Cathedral». 16th century Italian.*

*Chest-reliquary made of bone. Late 10th century Spanish.*

*Closed altar-reliquary with the Annunciation by Zúccaro.*

*Altar-reliquary showing St Jerome at prayer by Zúccaro.*

*The Martyrdom of St Maurice and the Theban Legionary, by Romulo Cincinato (1542-1600).*

*St Cosmas and St Damian by Luis de Carvajal (1534-1607) and Navarrete, «El Mudo», (1526-1579).*

*St John and St Matthew by Navarrete.*

*St Agatha and St Lucy by Diego de Urbina.*

14. — Chapel: St Ambrose and St Gregory, Pope, by Diego de Urbina.

15. — Opposite: St Gregory of Nazianzus and St John Chrysostom, by Luis de Carvajal.

16. — Chapel: St Basil and St Athanasius, by Alonso Sánchez Coello.

17. — Opposite: St Bonaventure and St Thomas Aquinas, by Luis de Carvajal.

18. — Chapel: St Jerome and St Augustine, by Alonso Sánchez Coello.

19. — Chapel: Altar and carved image of Our Lady of the Consolation, Patroness of the Order of St Augustine.

20. — St Paul, first Hermit, and St Antony the Abbot, by Alonso Sánchez Coello.

21. — Opposite: St Lawrence and St Steven, martyrs, by the same painter.

22. — Lower choir: St Sixtus, Pope, and St Blaise, Bishop, by Luis de Carvajal.

23. — Lower choir: St Cosmas and St Damian, by Luis de Carvajal, drawn by Navarrete.

24. — St Mary and St Mary Magdalen, by Diego de Urbina.

25. — Opposite: St Vincent and St George, by Alonso Sánchez Coello.

26. — Chapel: Altar and carved image of Our Lady of Protection.

27. — Chapel: St Leocadia and St Engracia, martyrs, by Luis de Carvajal.

28. — Chapel: St Clare and St Scholastica, by Diego de Urbina.

29. — Chapel: St Agatha and St Lucy, martyrs, by the same painter.

30. — Chapel: St Cecilia and St Barbara, martyrs, by Luis de Carvajal.

31. — Chapel: St Paula and St Monica, widows, by Diego de Urbina.

32. — Chapel: St Catherine and St Agnes, martyrs, by Alonso Sánchez Coello.

33. — Chapel: Altar of Cristo de la Buena Muerte, carved life-size Crucifix.

*St Stephen and St Lawrence by Coello.*

*The Queen's Oratory. St Joachim, St Anne and the Virgin by Giordano.*

34. — St Martin and St Nicolas, Bishops, by Luis de Carvajal.

35. — Opposite: St Antony of Padua and Peter of Verona, martyr, by the same painter.

36. — Chapel: St Dominic and St Francis of Assisi, by the same painter.

37. — Chapel: Martyrdom of the eleven thousand Virgins, sketched by Tibaldi and executed by Juan Gómez.

38. — Chapel: St Benedict and St Bernard, abbots, by Alonso Sánchez Coello.

39. — St Bartholomew and St Thomas, apostles, by Navarrete.

40. — Opposite: St Barnabas and St Matthew, by the same painter.

41. — Altar of the relics: St Jerome in the Desert, by Federico Zúccaro, restored by Juan Gómez.

42. — St James and St Andrew, Apostles, by Navarrete.

43. — Opposite: St Simon and St Jude, Apostles, by the same painter.

All these paintings cost 291,061 reals.

*The King's Oratory. The Holy Family, copy of an original by Andrea del Sarto.*

*The Bishop's Chapel. Baroque altar.*

*The Sacristy. View of the chest of drawers.*

# THE SACRISTY AND PANTHEONS

## The Sacristy

This is a great hall that runs north — south, 30 metres long, eight wide and eight high up to the keystone of the vault. On the east side there are five windows on ground level alternating with four cupboards made of rich woods where the holy vessels and objects for the mass are kept. Nine more small windows high up on the cornice are matched by nine recesses on the west side. The vault was painted by Nicola Granello and Fabrizio Castello. A chest of drawers runs along the entire wall on the west side: it is made of acana, mahogany, ebony, cedar, terebinth, box and walnut.

The chest is crowned by a wonderful body in Corinthian style made of the same woods, leaving a broad table space in front for ornaments for daily service in the church. In the middle there is a fine mirror with a silver frame and rock crystal adornments — whose lines and colour clash with the austerity of the Sacristy —, a gift from Queen Marianne of Austria, and on the sides six smaller ones with silver plate adornments, finely fashioned by the Hieronymite lay friar Eugenio de la Cruz. The room is decorated with a selection of paintings.

The most notable picture in the Sacristy is the one covering the window lighting the altar of the Holy Family, by Claudio Coello, the last great painter of the Madrid school, which depicts the first service held at the Sacristy altar on October 19, 1684. The canvas shows a crowd of famous people portrayed with delicacy and skill: Charles II is kneeling in prayer before the Host, who holds in his hands Fray Francisco de los Santos, Prior of the Monastery; behind the King are Fray Marcos de Herrera, the grandees of the Court, the Dukes of Medinaceli and Pastrina, the Count of Baños, the Marquis of la Puebla and the eldest son of the Duke of Alba, and the Hieronymite community in two rows, singing. The portrait of the painter is the first figure with sideburns on the left looking at the painting.

*The Antesacristy, washstand and Pompeian vault decorated by Granello.*

*Altar of the
Holy
Sacrament.*

*The Adoration of the Host by Coello (1642-1693).*

*The Adoration of the Host (detail). King Charles II and his court.*

*Left door to the vestry of the Sacristy.*

White marble relief depicting Rudolph II of Germany giving the Host to the emissaries of Philip II of Spain.

◁ *The false prophet Balaam by Giordano.*

*Pantheon of the Kings.*

## The Pantheon of the Kings

13 steps lead down to a door with a composite order gilded bronze grille. Above the door a Latin inscription reads: "To Great and Almighty God. A holy place dedicated by the piety of the Austrias to the mortal remains of the Catholic Kings, who await the longed for day, beneath the High Altar, of the Restorer of Life. Charles V, most enlightened of Caesars, wished this resting place for himself and his line; Philip II, most prudent of Kings, chose it; Philip III, deeply pious prince, began the works; Philip IV, great in his clemency, constancy and faith, enlarged, embellished and finished it in the Year of Our Lord 1654".

34 more steps lead down part three landings. On the sides of the first are two false doors, and on the second two real ones leading to the Kings' charnel houses on the right — where María Cristina lies — and to the Infantes' on the left, where the dead bodies are deposited until they are completely dry and shrivelled, when they are transferred to their respective boxes in the pantheons. The staircase is lined with the finest marbles from San Pablo de los Montes and Toledo and jasper from Tortosa.

The Pantheon of the Kings is in the Baroque style, somewhat overloaded in comparison with the simplicity of the original Escorial foundations: it is of rich marble with a superabundance of gilded bronze. It is built between the foundations of the church, and the altar stone of the high altar is the keystone of the

*Marble funeral urns of the Queens.*

vault. This storey is in the shape of a polygon with sixteen sides. The diameter of the polygon is 10 metres; it is 5.68 metres high and 31 in perimeter. The floor is of Tortosa jasper with strips of marble from San Pablo de los Montes.

The altar, facing the main door, made of green Genoa marble, has a splendid, finely carved openwork gilded bronze frontal with a central bas-relief depicting the entombment of Christ, sculpted by Fray Eugenio de la Cruz and Fray Juan de la Concepción, Hieronymite lay friars of the Monastery. The gilded bronze angels were made by Clemente Censore of Milan; the chandelier by Virgilio Fanelli of Genoa; and the altar crucifix, which is of little worth, by Domenico Guidi. The altar of the Pantheon is crowned with a tympanum divided by a central bronze cartouche on which we can read: Resurrectio nostra. The eight larger sides of the wall are occupied: one by the door; the one opposite by the altar; and the six remaining ones, three on either side, by twenty-four brown marble funeral urns, 1.78 metres long, 84 centimetres high and 70 wide. They all rest on four gilded bronze lion's claws. In the centre of the urns, on a gilded bronze cartouche in raised black lettering, may be read the name of the king or queen whose remains it contains.

On the right of the altar are the urns of the kings and on the left those of the queens whose sons have been kings of Spain. The only exception to this rule was Queen Isabel of Bourbon, Philip II's first wife, buried here at the express wish of that Monarch.

## Kings

Charles V, Emperor (1500-1558)
Philip II (1527-1598)
Philip III (1578-1621)
Philip IV (1605-1665)
Charles II (1661-1700)

Luis I (1707-1724)
Charles III (1716-1788)
Charles IV (1748-1819)
Ferdinand VII (1784-1833)
Alfonso XII (1857-1885)
Francisco de Asís, King Consort (1822-1902)
Alfonso XII (1887-1941)

## Queens

Isabel, Empress (1503-1539)
Ana, fourth wife to Philip II (1549-1580)
Margarita, wife to Philip III (1584-1611)

*Gilded bronze chandelier decorated with beads made in Genoa by Virgilio Fanelli.*

Detail of the vault of the Pantheon of the Kings.

Isabel, first wife to Philip IV (1603-1644)
María Ana, second wife to Philip IV (1634-1696)
María Luisa, first wife to Philip V (1668-1714)
María Amalia, wife to Charles III (1724-1740)
María Luisa, wife to Charles IV (1751-1819)
María Cristina, fourth wife to Ferdinand VII (1806-1878)
Isabel II (1831-1904)

The only absent kings are Philip V (1683-1746), who is buried at La Granja with his wife Isabel of Farnese; and Ferdinand VI (1713-1759), buried in the Salesas Reales in Madrid with this wife Barbara of Braganza.

*Pantheon of the Infantes. Gallery.*

## The Pantheon of the Infantes

Returning to the fork in the staircase and going down to the right past two landings, we reach the entrance to the Pantheon of the Infantes. Through the door of the Pantheon, on the last landing, there is a window on the left and a door on the right leading to a charnel house containing the remains of Antonio of Orleans and an Infanta, the daughter of María Eulalia and Antonio of Orleans who was born dead on March 12 1890.

The architect of the Palace, José Segundo de Lema, was in charge of the project, which was approved by Isabel II on January 7, 1862. The marbles of the dado are from Portor and Cuenca; and those of the bays from Carrara. Ponciano Ponzano, a sculptor, modelled the heralds, the sculptures and the adornments and they were carved in Carrara in marble from that city by the Italian sculptor Jacopo Baratta di Leopoldi. Work was suspended from the revolution in 1868 until Alfonso XII ordered its resumption in May 1877 and gave five thousand pesetas a month. It was completed on March 1 1888.

It cost one million seventy-five thousand three-hundred and six pesetas and sixty centimes, not counting the sepulchres of the sisters of Alfonso XII, which were built later.

There are nine burial chambers: five beneath the Sacristy, one beneath the Prior's Cell and three beneath the Chapterhouses. The floors are made of white Carrara and grey Bardiglio marble and the walls are lined with Florentine marble with white strips of Carrara. Each chamber has its altar of selected marbles.

The altar painting, *The Descent from the Cross,* is by C. Cagliari, with a Valencia and Cabra marble frame and a porpyhry bead.

In the fifth chamber is the sepulchre of Don John of Austria (1547-1578), natural son of Charles V, conqueror of the Moriscos in Granada, of the Turks at Lepanto and Governor General of Flanders. It is in the centre of the chamber, crowned by a life size statue: he is full armour with the Golden Fleece and a sword in his hands. The statue was modelled by Ponzano and carved by the Italian sculptor Giuseppe Galleoti. The entire sepulchre is of white Carrara marble. The semicircular arch of the chapel is made of Florentine marble; the cross is of gilded metal.

The centre of the secret chamber is occupied by the Rotunda or Mausoleum of the Children, a work of middling artistic taste, a twenty-sided polygon built of white statuary Carrara marble on dark marble dados. It has 60 niches of which 32 are already occupied by princes and princesses who died at a tender age. The altar painting, by Lavinia Fontana, 1590, is a beautiful portrait of the Holy Family.

*Mausoleum of the child Infantes in Carrara marble.*

*St Luke the Evangelist by Juan Bautista de Monegro (1545?-1621).*

*Small temple in the Evangelists' Courtyard.*

# THE EVANGELISTS' COURTYARD

The four sides of the main Cloister enclose this splendid courtyard, one of the most beautiful and rounded parts of the buildings, which stretches 46 metres along each side. The architecture of the façades is Doric in style on the first register and Ionic on the second, both of which have been built with care and grace. The 88 windows filling the spaces of the arches serve as an adornment. Above the second register, the courtyard is crowned by a pretty balustrade running all the way round. The courtyard itself is divided into squares decorated with box hedges and sown with flowers; there are four pools. In the centre, touching each pool, there is a beautiful small octagonal temple, one of Herrera's brilliant works, made of selected granite on the outside and lined on the inside with marbles from Espeja and Macael and serpentine from Granada with inlays, squares, strips and cornices. It is in Doric style and was exquisitely built. The outside is decorated with statues of the four Evangelists — St Matthew, St John, St Mark and St Luke — each in its niche of white Genoa marble, sculpted by Juan Bautista Monegro. Before each Evangelist is a marble figure of his symbol or allegory — the Angel, the Eagle, the Lion and the Bull —, and four small fountains feeding the four pools. The Evangelists are standing with books in their hands.

The
Evangelists'
Courtyard.

*Exhibition Room in the Library.*

## LIBRARY

The library is situated above the hall of the main portico, where we find the entrance on the right coming from Colonnade.

The entrance is framed by two fluted columns on which an inscription theatens those who take books or objects from the Library with excommunication. A door made of fine woods leads into a spacious hall 54 metres long, 9 wide and 10 high at the apex of the vault. The floor is of brown and white marble. Opulent Doric bookshelves run along the walls; they were designed by Juan de Herrera and made by Flecha, Gamboa, Serrano and other master carvers in

mahogany, ebony, cedar, orange wood, terebinth and walnut and rests on a Spanish marble socle. In the middle of the hall is a wooden armillary sphere, carved and painted in Florence in 1563 and five square marble tables with bronze edges dating from the foundation. Between them stand two octagonal porphyry pedestal tables, the gift of Philip IV. The hall is well lit by five windows and five balconies giving onto the Kings' Courtyard and another seven large windows opening onto the east Colonnade. The bookshelf alone cost 13,000 ducats. The hall is divided into three sections by two protruding arches with matching pilasters. Against the pilasters, between two columns of the bookshelf, are four life size por-

traits: the Emperor Charles V, Philip II and Philip III, painted by Juan Pantoja de la Cruz; and Charles II, by Juan Carreño de Miranda.

A superb half-length portrait of the historican of the Monastery and classic writer, Fray José de Sigüenza, hangs above a 16th century chest in the first of the east facing windows. In other windows there are portraits of Arias Montano and Francisco Pérez Bayer, tutor to the children of Charles III; a Roman bust found in the excavations at Herculaneum; another, in plaster, of the famous sailor Jorge Juan; and two reliefs in the same material which show the two sides of the medallion of the architect Juan de Herrera made by the lapidary Giacomo di Trezzo.

The tables and pedestal tables of the Library house exhibitions of books behind glass: ''The Apocalypse of St John'', all the pages illuminated and painted in miniature; ''The Prayer Book of Isabel the Catholic''; ''The Prayer Book of Queen Margarita of Austria''; ''The Breviary of the Emperor Charles V''; ''The Breviary of Philip II, illuminated by the Hieronymite monks of the Escorial and Ambrosio de Salazar; ''The Capitulary of the Escorial'', illuminated by Fray Andrés de León; a ''15th century Roman Missal''; ''The Breviary of the Catholic Kings''; Charles V's ''Officium Salomonis'', written for his voyage from Flanders to Spain by the Ghent printer Robert de Keysere and illuminated by his sister Clara; ''The Book of Hours of the Zuñigas''; ''The Koran'' of Muley Zidán, Sultan of Morocco, and other Arab and Persian books, as well as a ''Hebrew Bible''; ''A 14th century Holy Bible''; ''Le Jouvencel'', an allegoric, historical and military novel of the 15th century; ''The Breviary of Love'', in ancient Provencal verse of the 14th century; ''The Imitation of Christ'' in Mexican; ''Trojan Chronicle'', from the 14th century; ''Pliny'', in Italian, from the 15th century; ''Of the baptism of St Augustine'', from the 7th century; ''Three books of the Maxims of St Isidore'', which belonged to Alfonso II, the Chaste, ''The Apocalypse'' by Beatus of Liébana, from the 9th century; the ''Golden

Codex'' of 1043, so called because it is all written in letters of gold, which contains the four Gospels with prefaces by St Jerome and the canons of Eusebius of Caesarea; the ''Vigilian Codex'', or Albeldense, in which the general and particular councils of Spain, France and Africa were copied; ''The Papal Decrees''; the ''Book of Laws''; ''The Chronicle of Albelda'', by the monks of Albelda, Vigila, Sarracido and García,

which were completed in 976; a ''Genealogical chronicle of kings'', up to the Catholic Kings, in Latin; ''General heraldry and the origin of the nobility'', by the Cardinal Archbishop of Augsburg, Otho Truchsess, dedicated to Philip II; ''The Cosmography of Ptolemy'', from the 15th century; the ''Book of drawings, monuments and antiquities of Rome and Italy'', in ink and gouache, by Francisco de Holanda,

*The Emperor Charles V's breviary. 16th century parchment codex, Flemish school.*

*Fray José de Sigüenza, 17th century Spanish school, attributed to Juan Pantoja de la Cruz and Coello.* ▷

a 16th century Portuguese writer of treatises on Art. Works by Alfonso X, the Wise: "The Canticles of St Mary", beautifully written with splendid miniatures, from the end of the 13th century; the "Fifth part of the Great General History", from the library of Isabel the Catholic; "Games of chess, dice and backgammon", written in Seville in 1262; "The Lapidary", or the properties, sizes and colours of stones, from the 13th century; and the "Books of Astronomical Knowledge", copied at the orders of Philip II for the instruction of Prince Charles, with drawings by Juan de Herrera; "The Ordinance of Alcalá", a copy made for King Peter I of Castile, and a manuscript of "The Coronation of the Kings", from the 14th century.

Here too are manuscripts by St Teresa of Avila written in her own hand: "The Life", "The Way of Perfection", and the "Book of Foundations". The Saint's writing desk is also kept in the Library.

"Don Juan Dacosta's "Roman Breviary", from the 14th century; another, from the same century; a "14th century Missal"; Eliano's "Military Tactics", in Greek, written and illuminated for Philip II; "The Exposition of the festivals of the Greek church", by Juan de Euchaita, also written and illuminated by Nicolás de la Torre for Philip II; and "Hymns in praise of the Virgin", also in Greek, with illuminations in Byzantine style, from the 14th century. There are also examples of Arab and other artistic Spanish bindings of the 14th century, in gold, polychrome, etc., and bindings of Philip II and Don Diego Hurtado de Mendoza, and two incunabula: one from Zaragoza, 1481, the only copy; and another from Valencia, 1475, which is the most ancient Spanish example in the Library.

## History of the Library

The library was founded by Philip II, a true protector of the arts and sciences, as anyone visiting the priceless treasures of the Escorial can see.

*Benito Arias Montano, attributed to Zurbarán (1598-166...).*

D. B.ᵀᵛˢ ARIAS MONTA
VIR INCONPARABILIS

The first stock was 4,000 volumes presented by Philip II from his private collection, among which were manuscripts in many languages, notable for their binding in black or purple Morocco leather on board, with his arms engraved on the centre. The first batch were delivered in 1575, and catalogues of the printed works and manuscripts, compiled as they were received, still survive.

At the beginning of 1576, Don Diego Hurtado de Mendoza donated his own rich collection to Philip II, who accepted it on condition that he paid all debts and obligations in Mendoza's will.

Moreover, more manuscripts and printed books were brought by Philip's orders: 130 volumes from the Royal Chapel in Granada; 94 from the estate of Don Pedro de León, Bishop of Plasencia; 234 manuscripts and printed works from the Aragon historian Jerónimo de Zurita; 87 from Doctor Juan Páez de Castro, the chronicler of Charles V and Philip II; 293 collected from Mallorca, Barcelona and the monasteries of Murta and Poblet, many of them works by Ramon Llull; 31 manuscripts from Don Diego González, Prior of Roncesvalles; 130 works of those which Serojas had from the King; 139 from the Inquisition; 45 which Don Alonso de Zúñiga presented to the Library; 206 donated by Arias Montano, among which were 76 Hebrew manuscripts; 486 from the library of the Marquis of Vélez; 933 from the estate of the Cardinal of Burgos, Don Francisco de Bovadilla y Mendoza; 135 from Don Antonio Agustín, Archbishop of Tarragona, most of them Latin manuscripts; and many others given by private individuals, notable among which, for their antiquity and value are those given by Doctor Burgos de Paz and Don Jorge de Beteta.

All of them were classified by Arias Montano, assisted by Fray Juan de San Jerónimo and other monks of the Escorial.

In 1609 the books of Don Alonso Ramírez de Prado were added; they were acquired by Philip II for the

*Trojan chronicle. 14th century parchment manuscript which belonged to Isabella the Catholic.*

royal treasury. Later he enriched the Library with the collection of Muley Zidán, Sultan of Morocco, consisting of over 3,000 Arabic manuscripts. At some time or other, some of the manuscripts kept in the famous library of the Count-Duke of Olivares were also brought there.

Philip II assigned a fixed amount for upkeep and repairs and new acquisitions; this was increased in the reign of Philip IV to the sum of about 2,000 ducats per year. The privilege of the gift of one copy of every book printed in Spanish domains was also granted, and in 1619 its observance was recommended to the Viceroys of Naples, Milan, Sicily, Flanders and other kingdoms; this privilege was confirmed by successive kings.

With such elements and protection, the Library of the Escorial should have been one of the first in Europe, not only for the number of books, but also for the value of the collection, but, unfortunately, this was not the case. The privilege of acquisition of books was not observed because of the negligence of those responsible, and later it was totally annulled, and just a few donations trickled in.

On top of this came the disastrous fire of 1671 which consumed more than 5,000 manuscripts and many books, and the transfer to Madrid of much of the collection by Napoleon's invading Government. Between 1820 and 1823 losses were suffered, and various manuscripts disappeared. In 1859 there were about thirty thousand volumes to which were added, by royal decree on May 1 1876, the books of the so-called Seminary Library, founded by the blessed Antonio María Claret, outgoing Archbishop of Cuba and then President of San Lorenzo, which amounted to about forty thousand books and 2,000 manuscripts in Arabic, 2,090 in Latin and the vulgate, 72 in Hebrew and 580 in Greek.

One feature of this Library is the disposition of the books with the spine inward. This ensures that fewer are damaged when they are taken out or replaced, since the spine is less bulky, and the gilded page edges look more elegant, brighter and more sumptuous than the brown monotony of the cowhide spines, which are bare of labels or adornments.

*New Testament. 12th century Greek codex with Byzantine decoration.*

*Breviary of the Catholic Kings. 15th century parchment codex.*

*Paradise, Purgatory and Hell. 16th century tapestry from Brussels from a painting by Bosch.*

# THE TAPESTRIES

Tapestries are one of the most important elements in decoration, so it is natural that there is no lack of them in the Monastery of the Escorial, especially considering that Philip II was one of the main contributors to the splendid collection of tapestries, one of the finest in the world, which comprises the former collection of the Crown, now the property of the Nation. The ancient inventories show that Philip II did not order tapestries to be specially manufactured for the Monastery, but he did designate a number of Series of the great Collection to be hung in various parts of the Escorial.

And so, in the Delivery Book we find draperies I, II and III of Series 3, which are: *The Crucifixion, The Maries meeting Jesus, The Eternal Father with the World in his Hands.* Two of the Series of the Life of

the Virgin: *The Adoration of the Child* and *The Nativity* and, finally, *The Mass of St Gregory,* one of the most ancient tapestries in the Collection which belonged to Isabel the Catholic.

We cannot be certain if these tapestries remained for long hanging on the walls or if they were hung on special occasions. However, we can be certain that in The Ambassadors' Room there were various opulent embroidered canopies which no longer exist, though those tapestries are preserved in the Crown Collection, which leads us to suppose that there were not on show for long.

Now the tapestries that made up Charles V's Canopy have been hung once more in the Ambassadors' or Throne Room; it consists of a central drape representing the Crucifixion, and the roof of the Canopy, where the Eternal Father is depicted. Contemporary documents tell us that this was the canopy used by the Emperor when he abdicated in Brussels.

*The Ambassadors' Antechamber. Tapestries by Goya, Bayeu and Castillo, Empire style chairs and Sèvres jars.*

*The kite (detail) from a cartoon by Goya (1746-1828).* ▷

Also on show in the Throne Room are two of the drapes of the Spheres Series, which passed from the Crown of Portugal to the Crown of Spain on the marriage of Philip II to Maria of Portugal. These are magnificent tapestries woven with metals depicting The Earthly Sphere held up by Hercules and The Armillary Sphere by Atlas.

But the finest tapestries in the Escorial are to be found in the Bourbon Palace and date from the 18th century. King Charles III's large family meant an extension of the royal apartments, and all the rooms giving onto the Coach Courtyard and the west façade as far as the Battle Gallery were refurnished and redecorated.

This was the zenith of the Royal Tapestry Works in Santa Barbara. The Bayeu brothers, José del Castillo and Goya were the painters who did the cartoons from which the tapestries were woven; heroic, mythological and religious subjects were discarded in favour of scenes depicting popular life and customs. Here are the Majas, the dandies, the bullfighters, the street vendors; all these characters who appear in the comedies of Moratín, Don Ramón de la Cruz and others.

From surviving documents we know that in the Royal Works the tapestries were woven for the different rooms where they were to hang: the Royal Oratory, the Audience Chamber, the bedrooms, the Dining Room, etc.

Those tapestries were small and were attached to the

The Ambassadors' Room.
Tapestries by Bayeu,
Empire style furniture and
ceiling decoration by
Felipe López.

Woman drawing water
from a well, tapestry
from a cartoon by Teniers
(1610-1690).

*The sausage maker Pedro Rico from Candelario, from a cartoon by Bayeu (1746-1793).*

*Picnic at the Cherry Tree Inn from a cartoon by Bayeu.*

*State Banqueting Hall. Tapestries by Goya, Bayeu, Castillo and Anglois.*

The washer-women, cartoon by Goya.

The maja
and the
cloaked
men,
tapestry also
known as
"A walk in
Andalucía"
from a
cartoon by
Goya.

Boys climbing a tree, cartoon by Goya.

*Dogs on a leash, cartoon by Goya.*

*First antechamber or Rubens Room, with tapestries of the "Adventures of Telemachus" from drawings by the artist.*

*The Shipwreck of Telemachus*, tapestry whose drawing is attributed to Rubens whilst the cartoon is by Houasse.

Second antechamber
with tapestries by Anglois
in imitation of
Wouwerman.

Part of the Antechamber
to the Banqueting Hall,
with tapestries by Teniers
and Wouwerman.

*Calvary, Flemish tapestry from the early 16th century belonging to "Charles V's Canopy".*

Corner of the Pompeian Room with female figures in cameo and sofas, chairs and braziers in Ferdinand VII style.

Audience Room or Reception Room with Neogothic style furniture and tapestries by Bayeu, Teniers and Castillo.

The game of petanque,
cartoon by Bayeu.

First bedroom or Music
Room, tapestries by
Bayeu, Anglois and
Teniers and Empire and
Neogothic style furniture.

*The Earth protected by Jupiter and Juno, early 16th century Flemish tapestry, from the "Spheres" series.*

walls framed in gold or white and gold. The rooms were hung with all those scenes whose familiarity in no way detracts from their grace and beauty. From cartoons by Goya, we have: *The pottery seller, The Maja and the cloaked men, The kite, The boys picking fruit, The swing, The washerwomen, The sunflowers, The dance on the banks of the Manzanares, The fox hunt, The boar hunt, The fight at the new inn, The game of bat and ball, The child with the lamb, The toy bull, The lady and the soldier, The grape harvest, The child and the bird, The game of cards, The pack of dogs, The children blowing up balloons, The quail hunt* and *The amateur bullfight.* Some of these are repeated, as are some of those by Bayeu and Castillo.

Bayeu's tapestries are: *The coach game, The sausage maker, The Paseo de las Delicias, The children playing bullfights,* and *The game of cards.* Castillo has left not only popular scenes but also scenes from the classics. Among the first kind are *The return from the hunt, The Paseo del Retiro, The hare hunt, Ladies playing the tambourine, The fisherman, Still life with game, Woman selling peppers;* of the second, the so-called *Pompeians* and the *Dance of the Nymphs.* There is another series besides which is outside the area of popular scenes which was woven from cartoons attributed to Houasse: the *Life of Telemachus.* The set gracing the rooms of the Palace of the Bourbons would be hard to match for beauty.

*The Hall of Honour with Van der Weyden's Calvary at the background.*

*Panorama of the Monastery with "Philip II's Seat" in the foreground.*

## CURIOUS FACTS ABOUT THE MONASTERY OF THE ESCORIAL

The Monastery of San Lorenzo el Real de El Escorial is situated on a shoulder of the Sierra Carpentera, 1028 metres above sea level; 52 kilometres from Madrid, which can be seen on clear days from the east side; latitude 40°, 35', 25'' and longitude 5°, 29', 10'' on Paris longitude 0°. The meridian of the building has a declination to the West of 12°, 16', 19'', an error in orientation which may be due to the cardinal points having been shown on a compass whose magnetic needle, at the time when the Monastery was built, had a declination of about 12° east.

Immediately to the north of the Monastery is San Lorenzo de El Escorial, a town of 6,300 inhabitants; while to the east, in a dip, is the village of El Escorial, which gave its name to the Monastery.

The Monastery is flanked by mountains to the north and west, and to the south and east a broad, beautiful horizon stretches away. The sky is blue and clear; the climate is mild, except on the winter days when the gale blows. The land around abounds with leafy woods and clumps of rockroses, and there are many springs of fine, pure water.

The Monastery forms a rectangular parallelogram whose sides measure 207 by 161 metres. The material used in the building is granite; the predominant style is Doric; the roofs are covered with slate and lead sheets; and the eight towers and the dome enhance its beauty and grandeur.

The building, imposing in its size, conforms to Graeco-Roman canons of style, somewhat austere and dry for want of ornamentation.

"The Monastery of El Escorial", wrote one author, "is as majestic and sublime as the religion that brought it into being; as severe and melancholy as its august founder; a truly portentous work for the beauty and delicacy of its lines, for the justness of its proportions, for the felicitous combination of all its parts and the exquisite simplicity in which it rejoices in the midst of its very grandeur."

The construction works lasted twenty-one years: from April 23 1563 to September 13 1584. The building has 16 courtyards, 11 cisterns, 88 fountains, 13 oratories, 7 refectories, 9 towers, 15 cloisters, 86 staircases, 300 cells, more than 1,600 oil paintings and murals, 1,200 doors and 2,673 windows.

*South façade from the Convalescents' Gallery.*

*North and west façades.*

## THE LIFE OF THE ESCORIAL THROUGH HISTORY

Once Philip II's funeral had been held in Madrid, the new King returned to San Lorenzo and spent the feast of St Jerome there (September 30) and several days hunting, his burning passion.

The following year, accompanied by his wife Queen Margarita of Austria, he was received with great solemnity: the whole House had been lit up. On October 22 1600, in the presence of the royal personages, the last bronze funeral statues of Charles V and Philip II and their wives, sisters and children were placed above the royal oratories in the presbytery, replacing the gilded and painted plaster figures. In the same year the festival of Corpus Christ was kept with great pomp and attended by the King and Queen.

Early in January 1601, Philip III was there hunting, and then left for Valladolid, where the court had moved. The cost at San Lorenzo had been no small one, since a whole host of courtiers had been housed there on their journey from Madrid to the new capital of the Monarchy.

From April to the end of July 1602, the court stayed at the Monastery: it was a summer blighted by constant heavy rain. In San Lorenzo, the time was spent in the parties, picnics, meals, games of cards and ball to which the weak, soft disposition of the young King was overly prone, to the considerable detriment of public affairs.

The codicile in Philip II's will concerning San Lorenzo had to be fulfilled to the letter and although the King wished and attempted to do so, he was opposed by his advisors, especially in the handing over of the two large estates of Campillo and Monasterio. In the end, the King and the Community agreed and in the summer of 1603 San Lorenzo, not without certain restrictions and annoyances, took possession of all its founder had left for it.

In the same year, on March 4 at nine in the evening, having reached a holy and still productive old age, the venerable lay Hieronymite Fray Antonio de Villacastín went to his rest. Although he was over ninety, his mind was as fresh and alert as when he was a boy. He never failed to keep the observances and laws in which he had been brought up with the utmost rigour. His funeral was like a royal one and was attended by many outsiders as well as every member of the communities of the Convent, the College and the Seminary.

Once its possessions were handed over, the community could administer his goods with complete freedom; by that time they amounted to some 60,000 ducats a year, to which Philip III later added a further 18,000. On May 22 1606, while serving his second term as Prior, the classic historian Fray José de Sigüenza died.

In 1612, more than 4,000 priceless Arabic, Turkish and Persian manuscripts were deposited in the Library. They had been the library of Muley Zidán, Sultan of Morocco, taken captive by Don Luis Fajardo, captain of the Spanish galleys. It was finally handed over in 1614. The main part of this collection was consumed by the flames in the fire of 1671. On October 3 1611 Queen Margarita of Austria died.

As Philip II had not left a pantheon worthy of the royal bodies, he charged his children with the task of housing his bones and those of his parents, arguing that he had done his part by building the House of God. Philip III, eager to carry out this charge, ordered work to begin in 1617 according to the plans of the architect Juan Gómez de Mora. When the pantheon was nearing completion, Philip III died in Madrid, on May 31 1621, and work was suspended.

Philip IV tried, at the beginning of his reign, to build a palace and adorn it with fountains and gardens, a concept that finally became reality at the Buen Retiro in Madrid. The King was offered the nearby Campillo

*The Throne Room.*

meadow, which had been left to the Monastery by Philip II, as a suitable site for his project. The all powerful favourite Count-Duke of Olivares suggested to the Community that they might cede the ground, but he met with a refusal. Olivares was annoyed and sued the convent, but he lost thanks to the integrity and firmness of the energetic Prior, Fray Martín de la Vera. The favourite made a last appeal to the power of the King who touched the clothes that he was wearing and told his minister: ''Have no illusion, those estates belong to the monks, just as these clothes belong to me'', thus putting an end to a tiresome affair.

In 1625 Philip IV came to show the Monastery to the Prince of Wales, Charles Stuart, whom he tried to marry to one of his sisters.

In August 1638 Philip IV endowed San Lorenzo with an annual income of 18,000 ducats in perpetuity: 10,000 for the monks and 8,000 for the Works, with an obligation to add five more anniversaries to those already existing, with then daily masses to be said: six for him, two for his wife and two more for his brother, the Infante Prince Charles. The convent was also to choose two more monks to accompany those who already kept the vigil before the Sacrament, a father and a lay brother, so that when the choir was empty, four monks would be praying night and day in perpetual adoration of the All Holy.

The following year, on July 7, the convent graciously offered the King two more daily masses, having received this paper which Philip IV wrote to the Count-Duke of Olivares.

"Count: The guest whom I brought to my house; the time in which we are living; the infallible certainty that we are mortal, and the power of the divine services for the redemption of guilt, have made me more keenly mindful that some day this life must end; and supposing that this is so, and that by God' mercy I have been granted more power than other men, it has occurred to me to ensure that in all the convents in my kingdoms it shall be arranged that each day one or two masses, or more according to the capacity of each place, be said for my soul, and since they are many, it appears that the number of masses at the end of the year will be great; and at least we shall have this prior relief. See how this can be arranged, and if it should be needful to inform some minister to look to its prompt and speedy execution, you will do so, for there can be no doubt that for me it will be the greatest, most agreeable and most beneficial service which I shall have received at your hands, which have already performed so many and such great ones."

On October 9 1649 the Monastery was lit up with 12,000 lights to receive Queen Marianne of Austria, whom Philip IV had taken as his second wife.

Work on the pantheon, halted since the death of Philip III and almost destroyed by the dampness of the ground, which corroded the marbles and coated the bronzes with mould, began again under the supervision of a royal intendant who, from Madrid, gave orders and spent money and time without managing to dry out the site. So it would have to be built elsewhere, but the vicar of the convent, Fray Nicolás de Madrid, advised by the two famous silversmiths Fray Eugenio de la Cruz and Fray Juan de la Concepción, lay brothers of San Lorenzo, presented a well thought out project to build it on the original site, overcoming the problems that had arisen there. Fray Nicolás' project was approved and he was named director of the works, which began on November 1 1645, with plans by the Italian Gian Battista Crescenzi, ennobled by Philip IV with the title of Marquis of la Torre; by His Majesty's chief architect, Alonso Carbonell; and by Pedro Lizargárate. The indefatigable monk soon disposed of the damp and channelled the water away at the insignificant cost of 602 reals. He breached the church wall so that the pantheon could receive sufficient, if not abundant, light. He built the present staircase and in nine years the work was finished, and the royal bodies were transferred with great solemnity to their new urns after a splendid funeral in the main church, graced by the presence of the King.

Fray Nicolás de Madrid was raised to the bishopric of Astorga as a reward for his merits, and the humble lay brothers Fray Eugenio and Fray Juan were rewarded by Philip IV, who granted them a generous annual pension.

Philip IV, who often came to spend time at San Lorenzo, made the convent a present of the first game he killed. He sent a choice collection of paintings — described by Velázquez in his classic Memoir — which was hung in the Sacristy and the Chapterhouses; he repaired the capitals of two of the towers, which had been destroyed by lightning in 1642 and 1659; he increased the income of the Monastery by 13,200 ducats a year, in addition to the 18,000 already mentioned; he restored the cupola on the dome and enclosed the upper and lower main Cloister with windows. On January 17 1665 he died, to the great grief of the Hieronymites.

On June 7 1671, in the evening, a raging fire, fanned by a gale force wind, broke out in the College and then spread to the Monastery, turning the entire building into an immense bonfire. Thirty-eight bells in the organ tower melted, and the liquid metal flowed

*Exit vestibule or Room of Philip II's Sedan Chair.*

down the stairs. The only things to be saved from the flames were the Library, the Church and Philip II's apartments. More than 4,000 manuscripts were burned in the the main Cloister, where they had been put to save them from the fire. Herculean efforts managed to extinguish the fire on June 22. To repair the damage, Queen Marianne of Austria, the Regent, sent by royal warrant to all the justices for six leagues around, who came with all the able men they could find, each one carrying a basket, a spade or a hoe to help to remove the debris. They had to remain at San Lorenzo at their own cost until they were dismissed. The devastation was such that only 13 cells were habitable.

A Council was named to take charge of the rebuilding, but after several meetings they were still unable to reach agreement. Then, on May 29 1672, Fray Marcos de Herrera was elected Prior of San Lorenzo; he was well known at the court and gifted with a crystal clear intelligence and exceptional tenacity and energy. He became a member of the Council and finally became superintendent of the works. He demolished what had been rebuilt already, disregarding the 80,000 ducats which had already been spent, scrapped the Council's plans and accepted the proposal of the Toledo architect Bartolomé Zumbigo who, in a well written and well argued memorandum, answered the observations of the royal architect Peña and Olmo and justified his own method of reconstructing. The clashes and persecutions that Fray Marcos de Herrera had to endure were interminable, but the spirited prior did not take fright: he borrowed money, yoked over 300 pairs of oxen, spoke his mind and, with indomitable spirit, beat down and silenced the powerful, ruthless enemies who plotted against him at the court of the ailing, timorous Charles II.

In 1675 a ring of 32 perfectly tuned and toned bells was hung in one of the towers of the Kings' Courtyard; they had been cast in Flanders by Melchor de Hace for the Governor of the Low Countries, Don Juan Domingo de Haro y Guzmán, Count of Monterrey. In the autumn of 1676, when the rebuilding of the exterior of the Monastery was finished, Charles II came for the first time and was received with great ceremony: the building was lit with 14,000 lights. There were bullfights, hunts, fishing in La Fresneda; the Prior left out nothing which might please the Sovereign. It was on this visit that Charles presented the eyecatching rock crystal chandelier in the choir and a fine collection of pictures.

In December Father Herrera was summoned by the Monarch, who charged him with providing the fallen favourite Don Fernando de Valezuela, Marquis of Villasierra, with a refuge from his enemies in San Lorenzo. The Prior gave his word, though he had little reason to be grateful to the disgraced minister, and took him to the Monastery.

But the hate of his persecutors followed the toppled favourite and, convinced that neither force nor threats would persuade Father Herrera or the monks to give up the refugee after they had tried both in abundance, they violated the sanctity of the church and entered in warlike manner. The Prior's patience was at an end and he came down with the oldest monks to the high altar, performed the Holy Sacrament, which had never failed there since the days of the founder, and, showing no fear of that brazen armed troop, excommunicated the Duke of Medina Sidonia, Don Antonio de Toledo, the eldest son of the Duke of Alba, and all their accomplices and followers. They all had to travel to Rome to beg for absolution and the Pontiff, who had written a letter to the spirited Prior praising his course of action, imposed as a penance that they should build a chapel worthy of such a splendid work in the temple that they had profaned. Charles II came to the rescue by offering to intercede for the guilty men, and ordered the building of the altar of the Host, where the first service was held on October 19 1684, attended by the senior courtiers. This scene was immortalised by the brush of Claudio Coello in the beautiful painting which covers the recess where the precious relic hangs.

On May 22 1678, Fray Marcos de Herrera gave up the priory; by then all the fire damage of 1671 had been repaired. The rebuilding cost 802,100 ducats, of which the King put up 268,273 and the convent 533,827.

In 1690 Charles II came with his second wife, Queen Marianne of Neuburg, to inaugurate (on October 29) the completed altar of the Host. His reception was splendid: more than 36,000 lights illuminated the house. During his reign Giordano painted the frescoes on the main Staircase and the vaults of the church.

Charles II died in Madrid on November 1 1700, and the Hieronymites showed their gratitude to the king who had always been generous and liberal to San Lorenzo with unaccustomed masses of intercession. On June 24 1706 the troops of Archduke Charles came to the Monastery in an orderly and respectful manner; they were attended and warmly received by the monks, whom Philip V had ordered to swear fidelity in the event of his enemies' arrival.

In the Palace of San Lorenzo Queen María Luisa Gabriela of Savoy spent a night with her son Luis; they had fled from Madrid when the armies of the Archduke entered at the end of September 1710. Twelve years later La Granja was built, and San Lorenzo, which Philip V rarely visited as he was busy with the wars, took second place in the King's affections. On January 14 1724 Luis I was proclaimed King

*Ambassadors' Antechamber or Portrait Room.*

in the Monastery when his father abdicated.

From 1726 to 1731 the inner cloisters of the Monastery were enclosed with balustrades and glass windows.

In 1742 the skylight of the College was burned and two years later, on September 1, lightning set fire to the Company Quarters, burning, amongst other things, 3,000 bushels of flour, 10,000 of wheat, 6,000 of barley, 800 of oats and 120 of chick peas.

Philip V died in La Granja on July 9 1746 and was buried there. He was the first King not to be buried in San Lorenzo.

On November 1 1755 the Lisbon earthquake occurred at ten in the morning. The monks in the choir distinctly saw the chandelier sway for several minutes.

Ferdinand VI died on August 10 1759 and was interred in the Salesas Reales in Madrid.

At the beginning of Charles III's reign, the minister Grimaldi, in view of the inconvenience suffered by those accompanying the court for lack of lodging, suggested that the Hieronymites should build houses. The convent refused, "since it does not befit such a respectable Community to behave like an innkeeper"; but in 1776 they saw things differently and fulfilled the minister's wishes by putting up many new buildings.

In 1760 Fray Antonio de Pontones, a Hieronymite of La Mejorada and an excellent architect, built the underground passage, conceived by the Count of Montalvo, which crosses the north Colonnade.

The same year saw the beginning of work, according

*Philip II's apartments. Office and bedroom.*

to plans by Juan de Villanueva, on the Infantes' House. The Prince's and the Infante's Pavillions were begun in 1771 and almost at the same time the Hospital of St Charles, a theatre and a barracks were built. Finally the Ministers' House, which would enclose the Colonnade, was built in 1785. On October 8 1763 part of the slate roof of the Palace was burned; the repairs cost 450,000 reals.

In 1786, under the supervision of Villanueva himself, the construction of the House of the Spoken Mass in Madrid began. Today the building houses the Academy of History. At the time there were rumbles of protest at the exorbitant cost.

Charles III died on December 14 1788.

On June 25 1792, The Site, as the buildings adjoining the monastery had been known for many years, became a new village with its own boundaries, and in September of the same year, gained exemption from the jurisdiction of the village of El Escorial.

More than 18,000 spectators attended the General Chapter of the Order of Charles III, which was held in the presence of the court in the main church on the day of the Immaculate Conception in 1795. In 1799 the Community gave 4 hundredweight of silver to the Royal Treasury and, that same year on October 10 the priceless pectoral cross of rubies, diamonds, emeralds and pearls, valued at 40,000 ducats, that the prior wore at special festivals disappeared.

On March 19 1808 Charles IV abdicated in favour of his son Ferdinand VII.

On March 21 1805 Napoleon's troops appeared in San Lorenzo. While feigning friendship, they had taken possession of the main places in Spain. From March 29 to April 8 3,000 soldiers were lodging in the seminary.

On April 9 Ferdinand VII came and, after spending the night there, continued his journey to France. In may the invaders set up a field hospital and the Monastery had to give them 600 sheets, 200 stools and 600 shirts. When the outcome of the battle of Bailén was known, the French fled and on July 31 the populace sacked Godoy's palace, burning the statue of the favourite in front of the Infantes' House.

On September 18, Ferdinand VII, raising the banner three times, solemnly proclaimed the Prior of the Monastery royal standard bearer.

On October 9, the Prior and most of the Hieronymites fled; only 20 monks remained. On December 2, following on the heels of 22,000 Spanish troops who exhausted the ample provisions of the Monastery, 400 Frenchmen entered. Only three fathers remained in San Lorenzo.

On August 20 1809, the French sealed the doors of the main outbuildings and began systematically pillaging jewels, clothes, pictures and books. The statues of the Church reredos, except those of the top register, were trampled to the accompaniment of insults and sarcastic comments by Frederic Quillet, Napoleon's emissary, directed at the saints and the Hieronymites.

The magnificent Tabernacle was dismantled and taken to Madrid. To give an idea of what was stolen, in a single day 500 horses and 300 carts were requisitioned to carry objects to Madrid. The only things salvaged from this huge robbery were the monstrance of the Host, belonging to Charles II, and the Virgin of St Pius V, both hidden in the nick of time by Fray Pedro de Tomellosa.

The precious library was also taken to Madrid but, fortunately for Spain, Don José Antonio Conde, who was in charge of the removal, hid it among heaps of worthless papers in the convent of the Trinity, from where it was recovered in 1814, though not without some losses.

During 1812 various French and Portuguese — English armies passed through, causing no small damage.

On February 13 1814 the marble statue of St Lawrence was returned to its place above the pier of the choir with the fingers of the right hand broken and some of the bronze adornments missing.

On March 13 1814 replacement of the statues of the High Altar began. Benvenuto Cellini's Christ was replaced on March 19; Manuel Idiondo, a Basque stonemason, put back the arms, which had been taken to Madrid.

On June 14, at six in the morning, eight carts arrived with the Tabernacle, missing a few pieces. The fabulous inner monstrance had disappeared for ever. On July 7 188 books from the choir and some clothes were brought from Madrid and during the whole month more pictures, codices, documents and reliquaries were returned.

In 1826 a fire which lasted 18 hours destroyed the whole façade from the ladies' tower almost up to the church.

On January 10 1827 Fray José de la Cruz Jiménez was named Prior by the King. He was affable, if reserved and not especially learned, but he had a talent for getting on with people and, in spite of his reputation as a liberal, was an initimate friend of Ferdinand VII, who gave him 8 million reals for the restoration of the Monastery. Queen María Amalia gave a gold monstrance, gems and rubies, worth a million reals. The tabernacle was repaired and an inner recess made; the King gave 24 candlesticks, two incense burners with silver censers and spoons, a cross and six gilded bronze candle holders.

On August 10 1828, the Tabernacle was inaugurated. The Court had arrived some days before and been solemnly received with 40,000 lights. The frontals were stuccoed and the pulpits were made: these were valued — just the bronze work, not counting the marbles — at 15,000 pesetas. On September 29 1833 Ferdinand VII died in Madrid. The community offered him the same masses of intercession that they had performed for Philip II, and gave him the title of Restorer of San Lorenzo. The sumptuous pulpits that he had presented shortly before were used for the first time and from the Gospel pulpit Fray José de Quevedo spoke the funeral oration.

On December 1, all the monks, with more than 60 septuagenarians among them, were obliged to quit the convent where they had spent the best years of their lives, and found themselves alone and roofless in the street. Considerable consolation was provided in the form of the charitable welcome them by the inhabitants of the Site. The Hieronymites' goods were sold at public auction for 8,000 reals. At the beginning of 1838 the administrating abbot was put on trial and also forbidden to live in the Monastery. On the instructions of the Intendant, Don Pedro Egaña, on February 9 1847, the 16 chaplains were increased to 40 and were obliged to live in the Monastery.

Don Pedro Egaña's successor, Don José Peña Aguado, procured 1,500 pesetas a year for the conservation of the building, which was also in the solicitous care of the General Intendant of the Royal Household, the Marquis of Miraflores.

Father Claret was named President and Father Pagés Vice-President. A Royal Decree of November 14 1860 turned the ancient Hieronymite College into a secondary College where the pupils could study — apart from ecclesiastical subjets and primary and secondary education — Hebrew, Arabic, Greek, Latin, natural sciences, German, English, Italian, French, music, etc. The Rules, excellently set out by Father Pagés, were not approved by the Queen, and so he resigned from his post to be replaced by Don Dionisio González Mendoza, a serious, hard-working, energetic man with an extensive knowledge of both branches of the Law. He was the former ecclesiastical governor of Father Claret in the archbishopric of Santiago de Cuba.

Another Royal Decree of January 8 1861 reestablished the Seminary with 40 seminarists. These centres made giant strides. In 1865, 150 pupils enrolled in the Seminary: 72 free and 78 boarders, who paid five reals a day. The College had 121 students: 103 boarders and 18 day pupils. 30 priests taught the classes. The active hand of Father Claret, helped and supported by the indefatigable organiser Father Dionisio González, attended to every detail. He paved and whitewashed the inner cloisters; he took the manuscripts, to preserve them from the danger of fire, to the former linen room on the ground floor; he put gold frames on 70 large paintings, spent 70,000 reals on books, planted 10,000 fruit trees, laid 90,000 bricks in 1865 and installed 86,000 windows in two years, repaired the organs in the choir and made a small new one for the College Chapel, bought five pianos and a harmonium to study and acquired for the church 40 pairs of candle holders, 30 sets of gilded bronze sacring tablets, three large carpets and ornaments valued at 1,500 pesetas. In the college alone he spent more than 100,000 pesetas: he bought 300 iron beds with linen, 300 large and small tables, repaired four dormitories, two study rooms for 100 seminarists and 300 students, twelve classrooms with seats and teacher's chairs, and installed a fountain in like the one in the Monastery.

Even the Monastery houses in the Site were attended to and he built a new one for the guards, as well as a dovecote in the Company Quarters with 15,000 nests, a mill, the houses of Quejigal, Gózquez and Piul; he spent 70,000 reals on walnut, juniper, beech and pine for works and furniture. All this in less than five years. In June 1868 Father Claret resigned and Fray Rosendo Salvadó, Bishop of Nueva-Victoria, was named in his stead.

On August 10 1861, the railway opened; the first runs were made on June 24 in two trains which left Madrid at 7.10 in the morning. The following year work began on the Pantheon of the Infantes. At that time the annual income of the Monastery was about 726,000 reals.

The 1868 Revolution suppressed the Seminary, but wanted to conserve the College. Almost all the pupils were withdrawn by their families; just a few remained with some teachers, thanks to the selflessness of Father Pagés, who took over the direction.

Early in June 1869 Juan Manuel Zorilla, the monk, was named rector and the teachers from Father Claret's time left.

The Revolution of 68, which dethroned Queen Isabel II, nationalised Milanillo, El Castañar, La Granjilla, El Quejigal, Las Radas and Campillo.

Father Juan Manuel Zorilla, with people from his Corporation, opened the 1870 course.

By decree on January 14 1875, the Monastery of San Lorenzo was returned to the Royal Estates.

Early in August the same year, by order of the Palace, the Escolapian (charitable) Fathers left the Escorial. On the last course, they had had had 115 boarders. Of the distinguished Escolapians who taught at San Lorenzo, we should remember Father Manuel Mendia, the famous translator and annotator of the Summa of St Thomas Aquinas; Father Faustino Miguez, a man of great knowledge and proven virtue (who died on March 8 1925 at the age of ninety-four), well versed in the Natural Sciences, famous for his specifics, and founder of the nuns of the Divine Shepherdess, who provided free education for the humble classes; Father Felipe Vinuesa, general assistant, an excellent monk and mathematician; Father Antonio Ramos, teacher of Literature, a master of language and the author of various poems; Father Vicente Alfonso Salgado, librarian, a fine preacher, who later became Bishop of Cartagena, now deceased, etc.

When the Escolapians left, King Alfonso XII divided the building into three main parts: the Convent, the College and the Palace.

The Convent, dedicated to religious services and the observance of anniversaries and foundation masses, had 30 chaplains at whose head he placed the last Hieronymite Prior, Most Reverend Father Fray Jerónimo Pagés, a fine violinist and organist as well as a cultured man and lover of the Monastery.

The College was created on May 2 1875 and offered primary and secondary education, mainly for the orphans of army men, State and Royal Household employees, with 18 qualified teachers under the direction first of Don Agustín Romero, and then of the learned presbyter Don José Hospital y Tragó. His Majesty poured money into the College: he finished the physics and natural history sections, installed bathrooms and started riding classes, and left nothing out which might allow it to compete with the most advanced schools in Europe in hygiene and teaching material. He personally opened the course at the new centre on October 1 1879.

Two years earlier (May 25 1877), he had ordered the continuation of work on the Pantheon of the Infantes, which had been suspended since 1868. He paid for the arrears, the marble workshops were set up again and he allotted five thousand pesetas a month to finish the work quickly. It was completed down to the smallest detail on March 1 1888, but the King was already dead.

In 1885 King Alfonso decided to hand over the Monastery to a religious Order and, after various consultations, the order of St Augustine, in which at the time there was a flowering of science and literature, was chosen. the Augustines took possession of San Lorenzo on August 10 1885 and celebrated the inauguration with splendid festivals.

The Augustinians were also left in charge of the College and in 1886 they received the Library for their care and study.

On November 25 1885, when the King was only twenty-eight and at the start of his life, he died at the Pardo, and on the 29th the recently established Community and the pupils of the College received the body of their distinguished benefactor with due sad solemnity.

The restoration of the frescoes which had begun in

the previous reign proceeded under the child King Alfonso XIII.

In 1892 the Regent was recommended to convert the Company Quarters into a study centre; Queen Maria Cristina agreed with pleasure, and the necessary work was done at the expense of the Royal House, the Augustinian Fathers and the town of San Lorenzo. The old warehouses and offices of the Monastery housed more than 100 pupils with their teachers, inspectors and servants in comfortable quarters. On October 9 1893 the preparatory courses of Law, Philosophy and Letters, the first year of Jurisprudence, music, drawing and riding classes were inaugurated. The first rector was the Very Reverend Father Fray Francisco Javier Valdés y Noriega, later Bishop of Jaca and Salamanca. The new literary centre was called "the Maria Cristina College of Higher Studies" in honour of the august lady who had so generously protected the Foundation.

1896 saw the beginning of repair work in some of the Monastery outbuildings; fine collections of original paintings which had been scattered were formed in the Chapterhouses and the Sacristy; the lines of paving stones were replaced in the Colonnade; the flow of water was increased to reduce fire damage; and in 1901, in the Prior's lower cell, splendid jewels and art works were displayed in elegant showcases.

On February 10 1909, a fire burned part of the roofs of the College of Higher Studies, but repairs were carried out quickly and there was no need to interrupt the course.

In 1910 King Alfonso presented a beautiful embroidered cope, brought from Las Leandras in Seville, which is now kept in the Chapterhouses. The roofs of the Princes' Pavilion, unfortunately ruined, have now been returned to their pristine perfection, as have the frescoes in the Library, where the finest manuscripts to enrich this priceless literary treasure have been put on display in seven showcases.

He also ordered the rooms of Philip II and his daughters to be restored to their ancient, venerable state and work on them continued for several years, though with less success than might have been wished for art and history.

The surroundings of the Monastery were replanted with trees, turning the formerly bare and inhospitable area into beautiful pine woods and leafy forests. A dam of 300,000 cubic metres of water has also been built for the ever increasing population living around the ancient Monastery. Their Excellencies the Marquis of Morja (RIP) and the Count of Aybar, general Intendants of the Royal Household and Estates, worked tirelessly on these reforms.

Finally, early in 1930 work began on the installation of a magnificent electric organ to replace the old one in the choir, which was hardly ever used; it was built by Messrs. Eleizgaray and Co. of Azpeita (Guipúzcoa), and came into use in 1933.

*Philip II's sword, part of the armour called "Parade".*

*Philip II with the Order of the Garter
by Anton van Dashorst or Mor,
known in Spain as Antonio Moro
(1512/19-1575).*

# Contents

# Collection ALL EUROPE

Languages: Spanish · French · English · German · Italian · Catalan · Dutch · Swedish · Portuguese · Japanese · Arab

| # | Title | Sp | Fr | En | De | It | Ca | Nl | Sv | Pt | Ja | Ar |
|---|-------|----|----|----|----|----|----|----|----|----|----|----|
| 1 | ANDORRA | ■ | ■ | ■ | ■ | ■ | ■ | ■ | □ | □ | □ | □ |
| 2 | LISBON | ■ | ■ | ■ | ■ | ■ | □ | □ | □ | ■ | ■ | □ |
| 3 | LONDON | ■ | ■ | ■ | ■ | ■ | □ | □ | □ | □ | ■ | □ |
| 4 | BRUGES | ■ | ■ | ■ | ■ | □ | □ | ■ | □ | □ | □ | □ |
| 5 | PARIS | ■ | ■ | ■ | ■ | ■ | □ | □ | □ | □ | ■ | □ |
| 6 | MONACO | ■ | ■ | ■ | ■ | ■ | □ | □ | □ | □ | □ | □ |
| 7 | VIENNA | ■ | ■ | ■ | ■ | ■ | □ | □ | ■ | ■ | ■ | □ |
| 8 | NICE | ■ | ■ | ■ | ■ | ■ | □ | □ | □ | □ | □ | □ |
| 9 | CANNES | ■ | ■ | ■ | ■ | ■ | □ | □ | □ | □ | □ | □ |
| 10 | ROUSSILLON | ■ | ■ | ■ | ■ | □ | ■ | □ | □ | □ | □ | □ |
| 11 | VERDUN | ■ | ■ | ■ | ■ | ■ | □ | □ | □ | □ | □ | □ |
| 12 | THE TOWER OF LONDON | ■ | ■ | ■ | ■ | ■ | □ | □ | □ | □ | □ | □ |
| 13 | ANTWERP | ■ | ■ | ■ | ■ | ■ | □ | □ | □ | □ | □ | □ |
| 14 | WESTMINSTER ABBEY | ■ | ■ | ■ | ■ | ■ | □ | □ | □ | □ | □ | □ |
| 15 | THE SPANISH RIDING SCHOOL IN VIENNA | ■ | ■ | ■ | ■ | ■ | □ | □ | □ | □ | □ | □ |
| 16 | FATIMA | ■ | ■ | ■ | ■ | ■ | □ | □ | □ | ■ | □ | □ |
| 17 | WINDSOR CASTLE | ■ | ■ | ■ | ■ | ■ | □ | □ | □ | □ | ■ | □ |
| 18 | THE OPAL COAST | □ | ■ | ■ | ■ | □ | □ | □ | □ | □ | □ | □ |
| 19 | COTE D'AZUR | ■ | ■ | ■ | ■ | ■ | □ | □ | □ | □ | □ | □ |
| 20 | AUSTRIA | □ | ■ | ■ | ■ | ■ | □ | □ | □ | □ | □ | □ |
| 21 | LOURDES | ■ | ■ | ■ | ■ | ■ | □ | □ | □ | □ | □ | □ |
| 22 | BRUSSELS | ■ | ■ | ■ | ■ | ■ | □ | ■ | □ | □ | □ | □ |
| 23 | SCHÖNBRUNN PALACE | ■ | ■ | ■ | ■ | ■ | □ | □ | □ | □ | □ | □ |
| 24 | ROUTE OF PORT WINE | ■ | ■ | ■ | ■ | ■ | □ | □ | □ | □ | □ | □ |
| 25 | CYPRUS | □ | ■ | ■ | ■ | □ | □ | □ | ■ | □ | □ | □ |
| 26 | PALACE OF HOFBURG | ■ | ■ | ■ | ■ | ■ | □ | □ | □ | □ | □ | □ |
| 27 | ALSACE | ■ | ■ | ■ | ■ | ■ | □ | □ | ■ | □ | □ | □ |
| 28 | RHODES | □ | ■ | ■ | ■ | ■ | □ | □ | □ | □ | □ | □ |
| 29 | BERLIN | ■ | ■ | ■ | ■ | ■ | □ | □ | □ | □ | □ | □ |

# Collection ART IN SPAIN

| # | Title | Sp | Fr | En | De | It | Ca | Nl | Sv | Pt | Ja | Ar |
|---|-------|----|----|----|----|----|----|----|----|----|----|----|
| 1 | PALAU DE LA MUSICA CATALANA (Catalan Palace of Music) | ■ | ■ | ■ | ■ | ■ | ■ | □ | □ | □ | □ | □ |
| 2 | GAUDI | ■ | ■ | ■ | ■ | ■ | ■ | □ | □ | □ | ■ | □ |
| 3 | PRADO MUSEUM I (Spanish Painting) | ■ | ■ | ■ | ■ | ■ | □ | □ | □ | □ | ■ | □ |
| 4 | PRADO MUSEUM II (Foreign Painting) | ■ | ■ | ■ | ■ | ■ | □ | □ | □ | □ | □ | □ |
| 5 |  |  |  |  |  |  |  |  |  |  |  |  |
| 6 | THE CASTLE OF XAVIER | ■ | ■ | ■ | ■ | □ | □ | □ | □ | □ | □ | □ |
| 7 | THE FINE ARTS MUSEUM OF SEVILLE | ■ | ■ | ■ | ■ | ■ | □ | □ | □ | □ | □ | □ |
| 8 | SPANISH CASTLES | ■ | ■ | ■ | ■ | ■ | □ | □ | □ | □ | □ | □ |
| 9 | THE CATHEDRALS OF SPAIN | ■ | ■ | ■ | ■ | ■ | □ | □ | □ | □ | □ | □ |
| 10 | THE CATHEDRAL OF GERONA | ■ | ■ | ■ | ■ | ■ | ■ | □ | □ | □ | □ | □ |
| 11 | GRAN TEATRO DEL LICEO DE BARCELONA (The Great Opera House) | ■ | ■ | ■ | ■ | ■ | ■ | □ | □ | □ | □ | □ |
| 12 | THE ROMANESQUE STYLE IN CATALONIA | ■ | ■ | ■ | ■ | □ | □ | □ | □ | □ | □ | □ |
| 13 | LA RIOJA: ART TREASURES AND WINE-GROWING RESOURCES | ■ | ■ | ■ | ■ | □ | □ | □ | □ | □ | □ | □ |
| 14 | PICASSO | ■ | ■ | ■ | ■ | ■ | □ | □ | □ | □ | □ | □ |
| 15 | REALES ALCAZARES (ROYAL PALACE OF SEVILLE) | ■ | ■ | ■ | ■ | ■ | □ | □ | □ | □ | □ | □ |
| 16 | MADRID'S ROYAL PALACE | ■ | ■ | ■ | ■ | ■ | □ | □ | □ | □ | □ | □ |
| 17 | THE ESCORIAL | ■ | ■ | ■ | ■ | ■ | □ | □ | □ | □ | □ | □ |
| 18 | THE WINES OF CATALONIA | ■ | □ | □ | □ | □ | □ | □ | □ | □ | □ | □ |
| 19 | THE ALHAMBRA AND THE GENERALIFE | ■ | ■ | ■ | ■ | ■ | □ | □ | □ | □ | □ | □ |
| 20 | GRANADA AND THE ALHAMBRA (ARAB AND MAURESQUE MONUMENTS OF CORDOVA, SEVILLE AND GRANADA) | ■ | □ | □ | □ | □ | □ | □ | □ | □ | □ | □ |
| 21 | ROYAL PALACE OF ARANJUEZ | ■ | ■ | ■ | ■ | ■ | □ | □ | □ | □ | □ | □ |
| 22 | THE PALACE OF EL PARDO | ■ | ■ | ■ | ■ | ■ | □ | □ | □ | □ | □ | □ |
| 23 | ROYAL RESIDENCES | ■ | ■ | ■ | ■ | ■ | □ | □ | □ | □ | □ | □ |
| 24 | THE PALACE OF LA GRANJA | ■ | ■ | ■ | ■ | ■ | □ | □ | □ | □ | □ | □ |
| 25 | HOLY CROSS OF THE VALLE DE LOS CAIDOS | ■ | ■ | ■ | ■ | ■ | □ | □ | □ | □ | □ | □ |

# Collection ALL SPAIN

| # | Title | Sp | Fr | En | De | It | Ca | Nl | Sv | Pt | Ja | Ar |
|---|-------|----|----|----|----|----|----|----|----|----|----|----|
| 1 | ALL MADRID | ■ | ■ | ■ | ■ | ■ | □ | □ | □ | □ | ■ | □ |
| 2 | ALL BARCELONA | ■ | ■ | ■ | ■ | ■ | ■ | □ | □ | □ | □ | □ |
| 3 | ALL SEVILLE | ■ | ■ | ■ | ■ | ■ | □ | □ | □ | □ | □ | □ |
| 4 | ALL MAJORCA | ■ | ■ | ■ | ■ | ■ | ■ | □ | □ | □ | □ | □ |
| 5 | ALL THE COSTA BRAVA | ■ | ■ | ■ | ■ | ■ | □ | □ | □ | □ | □ | □ |
| 6 | ALL MALAGA and the Costa del Sol | ■ | ■ | ■ | ■ | ■ | □ | ■ | □ | □ | □ | □ |
| 7 | ALL THE CANARY ISLANDS, Gran Canaria, Lanzarote and Fuerteventura | ■ | ■ | ■ | ■ | ■ | □ | ■ | □ | □ | □ | □ |
| 8 | ALL CORDOBA | ■ | ■ | ■ | ■ | ■ | □ | □ | □ | □ | ■ | □ |
| 9 | ALL GRANADA | ■ | ■ | ■ | ■ | ■ | □ | ■ | □ | □ | □ | □ |
| 10 | ALL VALENCIA | ■ | ■ | ■ | ■ | ■ | □ | □ | □ | □ | □ | □ |
| 11 | ALL TOLEDO | ■ | ■ | ■ | ■ | ■ | □ | □ | □ | ■ | □ | □ |
| 12 | ALL SANTIAGO | ■ | ■ | ■ | ■ | ■ | □ | □ | □ | □ | □ | □ |
| 13 | ALL IBIZA and Formentera | ■ | ■ | ■ | ■ | ■ | □ | □ | □ | □ | □ | □ |
| 14 | ALL CADIZ and the Costa de la Luz | ■ | ■ | ■ | ■ | ■ | □ | □ | □ | □ | □ | □ |
| 15 | ALL MONTSERRAT | ■ | ■ | ■ | ■ | ■ | ■ | □ | □ | □ | □ | □ |
| 16 | ALL SANTANDER and the Costa Esmeralda | ■ | ■ | ■ | □ | □ | □ | □ | □ | □ | □ | □ |
| 17 | ALL THE CANARY ISLANDS II, Tenerife, La Palma, Gomera, Hierro | ■ | ■ | ■ | ■ | ■ | □ | ■ | □ | □ | □ | □ |
| 18 |  | □ | □ | □ | □ | □ | □ | □ | □ | □ | □ | □ |
| 19 |  | □ | □ | □ | □ | □ | □ | □ | □ | □ | □ | □ |
| 20 | ALL BURGOS, Covarrubias and Santo Domingo de Silos | ■ | ■ | ■ | ■ | ■ | □ | □ | □ | □ | □ | □ |
| 21 | ALL ALICANTE and the Costa Blanca | ■ | ■ | ■ | ■ | ■ | □ | □ | □ | □ | □ | □ |
| 22 | ALL NAVARRA | ■ | ■ | ■ | ■ | ■ | □ | □ | □ | □ | □ | □ |
| 23 | ALL LERIDA Province and Pyrenees | ■ | ■ | ■ | ■ | ■ | ■ | □ | □ | □ | □ | □ |
| 24 | ALL SEGOVIA and Province | ■ | ■ | ■ | ■ | ■ | □ | □ | □ | □ | □ | □ |
| 25 | ALL SARAGOSSA and Province | ■ | ■ | ■ | ■ | ■ | □ | □ | □ | □ | □ | □ |
| 26 | ALL SALAMANCA and Province | ■ | ■ | ■ | ■ | ■ | ■ | □ | □ | □ | □ | □ |
| 27 | ALL AVILA and Province | ■ | ■ | ■ | ■ | ■ | □ | □ | □ | □ | □ | □ |
| 28 | ALL MINORCA | ■ | ■ | ■ | ■ | ■ | □ | □ | □ | □ | □ | □ |
| 29 | ALL SAN SEBASTIAN and Province | ■ | ■ | ■ | ■ | ■ | □ | □ | □ | □ | □ | □ |
| 30 | ALL ASTURIAS | ■ | ■ | ■ | ■ | ■ | □ | □ | □ | □ | □ | □ |
| 31 | ALL CORUNNA and the Rías Altas | ■ | ■ | ■ | ■ | ■ | □ | □ | □ | □ | □ | □ |
| 32 | ALL TARRAGONA and Province | ■ | ■ | ■ | ■ | ■ | ■ | □ | □ | □ | □ | □ |
| 33 | ALL MURCIA and Province | ■ | ■ | ■ | ■ | ■ | □ | □ | □ | □ | □ | □ |
| 34 | ALL VALLADOLID and Province | ■ | ■ | ■ | ■ | ■ | □ | □ | □ | □ | □ | □ |
| 35 | ALL GIRONA and Province | ■ | ■ | ■ | ■ | ■ | ■ | □ | □ | □ | □ | □ |
| 36 | ALL HUESCA and Province | ■ | ■ | ■ | □ | □ | □ | □ | □ | □ | □ | □ |
| 37 | ALL JAEN and Province | ■ | ■ | ■ | ■ | ■ | □ | □ | □ | □ | □ | □ |
| 38 | ALL ALMERIA and Province | ■ | ■ | ■ | ■ | ■ | □ | □ | □ | □ | □ | □ |
| 39 | ALL CASTELLON and the Costa del Azahar | ■ | ■ | ■ | ■ | ■ | □ | □ | □ | □ | □ | □ |
| 40 | ALL CUENCA and Province | ■ | ■ | ■ | ■ | ■ | □ | □ | □ | □ | □ | □ |
| 41 | ALL LEON and Province | ■ | ■ | ■ | ■ | ■ | □ | □ | □ | □ | □ | □ |
| 42 | ALL PONTEVEDRA, VIGO and the Rías Bajas | ■ | ■ | ■ | ■ | ■ | □ | □ | □ | □ | □ | □ |
| 43 | ALL RONDA | ■ | ■ | ■ | ■ | ■ | □ | ■ | □ | □ | □ | □ |
| 44 | ALL SORIA | ■ | ■ | ■ | ■ | ■ | □ | □ | □ | □ | □ | □ |
| 45 | ALL HUELVA | ■ | ■ | ■ | ■ | ■ | □ | □ | □ | □ | □ | □ |
| 46 | ALL EXTREMADURA | ■ | ■ | ■ | ■ | ■ | □ | □ | □ | □ | □ | □ |
| 47 | ALL THE MONASTERY OF GUADALUPE | ■ | ■ | ■ | ■ | ■ | □ | □ | □ | □ | □ | □ |
| 48 | ALL ZAMORA | ■ | ■ | ■ | ■ | ■ | □ | □ | □ | □ | □ | □ |
| 49 | ALL PALENCIA | ■ | ■ | ■ | ■ | ■ | □ | □ | □ | □ | □ | □ |

# Collection ALL AMERICA

| # | Title | Sp | Fr | En | De | It | Ca | Nl | Sv | Pt | Ja | Ar |
|---|-------|----|----|----|----|----|----|----|----|----|----|----|
| 1 | PUERTO RICO | ■ | □ | ■ | □ | □ | □ | □ | □ | □ | □ | □ |
| 2 | SANTO DOMINGO | ■ | ■ | ■ | □ | □ | □ | □ | □ | □ | □ | □ |

# Collection ALL AFRICA

| # | Title | Sp | Fr | En | De | It | Ca | Nl | Sv | Pt | Ja | Ar |
|---|-------|----|----|----|----|----|----|----|----|----|----|----|
| 1 | MOROCCO | ■ | ■ | ■ | ■ | ■ | □ | □ | □ | □ | □ | □ |
| 2 | THE SOUTH OF MOROCCO | ■ | ■ | ■ | ■ | ■ | □ | □ | □ | □ | □ | □ |

The printing of this book was completed
in the workshops of FISA - Industrias
Gráficas, Palaudarias, 26 - Barcelona
(Spain)